Faith for Modern Times

*If your faith isn't working,
it's time to take another look.*

Brad W. Erlandson

Edited by Bralynn Newby

authorHOUSE®

AuthorHouse™
1663 Liberty Drive, Suite 200
Bloomington, IN 47403
www.authorhouse.com
Phone: 1-800-839-8640

First published by AuthorHouse   5/13/2009

ISBN: 978-1-4389-4916-1 (sc)

Printed in the United States of America
Bloomington, Indiana

This book is printed on acid-free paper.

Faith for Modern Times
by Brad W. Erlandson

*Unless otherwise indicated, Bible quotations are taken from
The Holy Bible: New King James Version, Compact Reference
Edition, Copyright © 1985 by Thomas Nelson, Inc.*

Table of Contents

Acknowledgements

This book has taken two years to complete. One of the reasons is I am presently in a wheelchair and everything takes longer. The other reason is that when the book was almost complete, I took it to a store to have some files transferred and the whole book was lost. My friend Jeff Tatarsky reminded me that Jeremiah had lost a book that he wrote too—God told him to write it again. That situation worked out pretty well for him, so I buckled down and wrote mine again too. This book is really born out of my own faith struggle; I hope it resonates with you. Many thanks also to my editor and friend Bralynn Newby. Without her work this book would not have been published.

Introduction

I entitled this book *Faith for Modern Times* because with all the talk about faith these days, it is important to learn how faith worked in the lives of Biblical people so that we can see how it applies to our lives today. This is not the final word, to be sure, it is only meant to stimulate thought in this area. As a zealous Christian it is easy to become confused when exposed to the many various teachings that seem to indicate that faith is a means to an end—usually financial or physical. In other words, if you had enough and have the right kind of faith you will have unlimited health and wealth.

When I was a young believer I was exposed to these teachings and because I wanted to know if this faith teaching was real, it created some unrest in me which led me to seek for the truth. I sincerely wanted the truth so I read and prayed and talked to people and went to church. When I heard the position that "faith people" took I was intrigued and excited to think that if I could reach a place of "activating" my faith I could literally move mountains. Literally.

I was taught in a formal theological setting for five years, which included studying Greek, eschatology and many central doctrines of the Christian faith. Yet when I was exposed to the "faith" teachings, I first thought that I had missed something. The faith teachers would always say that the Pharisees missed Jesus, though they knew the written text very well. Which meant that most college professors were Pharisees who were really missing the point, and in the final analysis—Jesus Himself. That's one thing I didn't want to do, so I would spend long hours making sure, through prayer and fasting, that I would in no way miss Him.

I have been a Christian for over 30 years and gone to Bible College and Seminary. In no way do I claim perfection, but I believe I have diligently sought the truth in this area. In fact, I taught Apologetics (the study of the defense of the Christian faith) in my local church. The issue of suffering would come up and even though I had been fed a steady diet of "if you have faith, you will not suffer" something in me didn't buy it. As I studied the scriptures it seemed that God never promised a suffering-free life no matter what level of faith you were on.

This research and study took on actual experience when in 2002 I was struck head on by a drunk driver and paralyzed from the waist down. At first my faith was high—God *will* heal me—but as of the writing of this book, without the assistance of braces, I cannot walk. This led me more and more to seek the truth. My previous book, *Walking This Walk* was written in light of this struggle.

Since I believe the scriptures to be the final word on faith and practice, I turned off most of what I was listening to in terms of teachers and preachers and began a search for myself as to what faith was and how it worked. I did read some authors that I trusted and still went to church, but my desire was to know the truth about faith. I use some authors in this book to compare and contrast various views of faith.

I look at four men in the Old Testament who walked with God over a lifetime. One thing really stood out to me and that was that faith, far from being a one shot deal—get a shot of faith for what you need, was something that was exercised toward God over a lifetime of peaks and valleys. Faith began with God, not men, because God was here first.

If that is the case then, God who? The book of Genesis says, "In the beginning God..." This is the God of the Bible; the God of Abraham, Isaac and Jacob, the God of the prophets, the God and Father of our Lord Jesus Christ. Not the God of Islam or the Buddhist idea of God or of the many offshoot cults who talk about God in ways that they can control. Contrary to us controlling God, or our faith controlling situations, it is He who has the final say.

Does God want us to have faith for things? Yes. Paul the Apostle said, "Be anxious for nothing, but in everything by prayer and supplication, with thanksgiving let your requests be made known to God" (Phil 4:6). Notice it says "supplications and requests", not "faith demands". For example, "God, you see my faith, therefore take this mountain (problem) and cast it into the sea." That being said we need to be persistent in prayer and to take God at His word and truly stand in faith for what we believe is God's will for us and our families.

The problem with the instant faith is, when what is "believed for" does not happen, immature and weaker Christians actually lose their faith as a result. If God doesn't work than what good is He—if He exists at all, they think. So this book, I believe is very important in bringing up the other side of what it means to believe God and to have genuine faith.

As I have struggled through this maze of being paralyzed and everything associated with it I find comfort in knowing that men of old, men of faith, held on during hard times. They continued to believe God in spite of their circumstances, because the focus of their faith was God Himself, not health or wealth. All four men I focus on did prosper financially and in other areas of their lives in the end, but there were seasons of hard places that forced them to determine what their faith was all about. Faith is a means to an end, and the end is God Himself. After all of Job's issues he concluded, "I have heard of You by the hearing of the ear, but now my eye sees You" (Job 42:5). He went from a place were he knew God through reading to knowing God through experience.

You may have picked this up as a new Christian, or you may have been walking with God many years. I hope, no matter where you are in your life, that you will really take the time to read and truly think about what is presented here. If you find yourself losing me, (which is most likely my fault) stay with it till the end. I think you will learn from these men and if nothing else be a more informed student of the Bible.

If you are going through a hard time right now and God is more of a mystery than ever, that is not necessarily a bad thing; God is teaching you and making you stronger as you persevere in faith. Don't ever let the lie of, "if you have true faith, you would not be sick or broke or in this unusual situation" cause you to become frustrated and confused. God is for you not against you. Contrary to this thinking it is the tests that come to us that teach us what true faith is all about. As I heard one man say, "You will never know you have faith, until you're in a good fight."

I pray that you are encouraged in your walk with God as you read. And as James says, "Count it all joy when you fall into various trials of many kinds" (James 1:2). Why? Because there is a very valid reason for them.

Chapter 1

Faith That Wrestles With God and Prevails

Jacob, the grandson of Abraham, is the first man I want to talk about. The first mention of him is before he was born.

"This is the genealogy of Isaac, Abraham's son. Abraham became the father of Isaac. Isaac was forty years old when he took Rebekah, the daughter of Bethuel the Syrian of Padan Aram, and sister of Laban the Syrian, as wife. Now Isaac pleaded with the Lord for his wife, because she was barren; and the Lord granted his plea, and Rebekah his wife conceived. But the children struggled together within her; and she said, 'If all is well, why am I like this?' So she went to inquire of the Lord. And the Lord said to her, two nations are in your womb, two peoples shall be separated from your body; one people shall be stronger than the other, and the older shall serve the younger" (Gen 25:19-23).

Here is an example of God's foreknowledge. God knew what was going to happen in regards to this particular situation. God was orchestrating the events surrounding the birth and growth of His people.

> "So when her days were fulfilled for her to give birth, indeed there were twins in her womb. And the first came out red. He was like a hairy garment all over; so they called his name Esau, [meaning hairy]. Afterward his brother came out, and his hand took hold of Esau's heel; so his name was called Jacob [meaning supplanter or deceiver]" (Gen 25:24-26).

Here is the prophetic word coming to pass. These are not just two babies; they are two heads of nations. One, God's chosen nation, the other is a head of a different nation. The boys are very different, Esau is a hunter, Jacob is a "mamma's boy" (Gen 25:27-29).

One day when the boys were older Esau came in from hunting and he was so famished he thought he was going to die. (I guess he didn't know you can go up to forty days without food.) Jacob, who was cooking stew, said that he would feed his brother if he sold him his birthright. "And Esau said, 'Look, I am about to die; so what is this birthright to me?'" (Gen 25:32). His birthright was the understanding that, as the first born twin, he would inherit the majority of his parents' estate, and would be considered the head of the remaining family. This is what he gave away or "sold" to Jacob. He would no longer be considered first born.

This is the beginning of bad feelings between Jacob and Esau, and they would eventually part ways. (So much for brotherly love.)

The custom of that day was for the father to ceremoniously pass the blessing on to his oldest son. In this case it would be a prophetic blessing for two nations. I will summarize what happened in Genesis chapters 27 and 28. Isaac believed he was dying so he called his firstborn, Esau (he did not know that Esau sold his birthright to Jacob), to give him his prophetic blessing (Gen 27:1-5). The plan was for Esau to go out to the field, hunt game, and cook the meat just the way Isaac liked it. Then he would eat it, give the blessing and die. Rebekah overheard Isaac tell Esau this and she told Jacob, her favorite. Their new plan would be that she would cook game the way Isaac liked, and then Jacob would serve it to Isaac and get the blessing. You see, Isaac was blind, so the only issue was that Esau had hairy arms, and Jacob did not. No problem for Rebekah though, a woman who was going to get what she wanted no matter what, even if she had to lie, cheat and steal. "And she put the skins of the kids of the goats on his hands and on the smooth part of his neck" (Gen 27:16).

Jacob beat Esau to his father, even though Isaac wondered if it was really Esau. "So Jacob went near to Isaac, his father, and he felt him and said, the voice is Jacob's voice, but the hands are the hands of Esau" (Gen 27:22). Jacob and Rebekah succeeded in stealing Esau's blessing. And it was an amazing blessing,

"Surely, the smell of my son is like the smell of a field which the Lord has blessed. Therefore may God give you of the dew of heaven, of the fatness of the earth, and plenty of grain and wine. Let peoples serve you, and nations bow down to you. Be master over your brethren, and let your mother's son bow down to you. Cursed be everyone who curses you, and blessed be those who bless you" (Gen 27:27-29).

So Esau comes home, and he and his dad realize that Jacob, true to his name—Deceiver, stole the blessing and it could not be recanted.

"'Have you only one blessing, my father?'... then Isaac, his father answered and said to him, 'Behold, your dwelling shall be of the fatness of the earth, and of the dew of heaven above. By your sword you shall live, and you shall serve your brother; and it shall come to pass, when you become restless, that you shall break his yoke from your neck'" (Gen 27:39-40).

Two blessings, and if you had to pick one, you would pick Jacob's. All this lying and deception is the set up for Jacob's departure from home and ultimately an encounter with Almighty God. Many times we think things have to be just right for God to show up, but as we shall see, this is not the case. Rebekah overheard that Esau was going to kill Jacob so she directed him to her brother's place in Haran, which was a good distance north. "Now therefore my son, obey my voice; arise, flee to my brother Laban in Haran. And stay with him a few days until your brother's fury turns away" (Gen 27:43-45). The plan was for Jacob to stay a few days but as it turns out, he is going to stay a lot longer than that. Rebekah gets Isaac to send Jacob off by telling him that she does not want him to take a wife from the daughters of the Hittites.

> "Then Isaac called Jacob and blessed him, and charged him and said to him, you shall not take a wife from the daughters of Canaan. Arise go to Paddan Aram...take yourself a wife from there of the daughters of Laban, your mother's brother (Gen 28:1-2).

Isaac sends him off with another blessing, "May God Almighty bless you, and make you fruitful and multiply you, that you may be an assembly of peoples; and give you the blessing of Abraham. To you and your descendants with you that you may inherit the land in which you are a stranger, which God gave to Abraham" (Gen 28:3-4).

In the midst of all this upset, pain, problems, lying, deception, anger, rage, and disappointment, God is speaking, giving blessing and direction. Again we think that circumstances have to be perfect for us to hear from God and that we have to be perfect as well. Many times it is in the turmoil of daily life with all of its issues that God speaks. When Jacob is in transit to Haran he gets something awesome from God.

"Now Jacob went out from Bersheeba and went toward Haran. So he came to a certain place and stayed there all night, because the sun had set. And he took one of the stones of that place and put it at his head, and he lay down in that place to sleep. Then he dreamed a dream and behold, a ladder was set up on the earth, and its top reached to heaven and there the angels of God were ascending and descending on it. And behold, the Lord stood above it and said: 'I am the Lord God of Abraham your father and the God of Isaac; the land on which you lie I will give to you and your descendants. Also your descendants shall be as the dust of the earth; you shall spread abroad to the west and to the east, to the north and to the south; and in you and in your seed all the families of the earth shall be blessed. Behold, I am with you and will keep you wherever you go, and will bring you back to this land; for I will not leave you until I have done what I have spoken to you'" (Gen 28:10-15).

Wow, can you imagine the God of the Universe speaking to you like that? *"I am with you wherever you go."* Jacob is still young and immature—you can tell by his response. After he rejoiced in the fact that God was in this place he made a "witness heap" (memorial to God) and he made a vow,

> "If God will be with me, and keep me in this way that I am going, and give me bread to eat and clothing to put on, so that I come back to my father's house in peace, then the Lord shall be my God. And the stone which I have set as a pillar shall be God's house, and of all that You give me I will surely give a tenth to You" (Gen 28:18-21).

I think you can approach this response from two ways. One, Jacob is immature and doubts God. God just told him point blank he would be with him, give him the land, bless his descendants and bring him back to the land. What kind of a response is this from Jacob? *"If* you give me bread and clothes and bring me back to my father's house, *then* you will be my God" (emphasis mine). Okay Jacob, you're basically telling God how it's going to go down. Prove yourself, and then if you do what I think you should do, I guess you will be my God. The other view is that Jacob knew what God was saying and was indeed wanting God to prove Himself. The question is what the word "if" means here. Many scholars would take this to mean a positive affirmation of belief, "if—and I know you will", and others would say that the word "if" is a statement of doubt. I think the doubting view is most accurate and speaks of our immaturity when we are young in age and/or in the faith. We somehow get the idea that God exists for us and He is obligated to bless us the way we think He should, and if He does then maybe we will continue to serve Him. Thankfully, God was very patient with Jacob, and was not upset with his (or our) immaturity or doubts, He understands, and will do what He says He will no matter what the level of our belief. It is going to take awhile, but the next time that Jacob meets God he will have a different response.

Jacob finally gets to Laban's place. The first person he meets is Laban's daughter, Rachel, his cousin. After talking to Laban, Jacob stays with him for about a month. Laban says to Jacob that he should not serve him for nothing just because they are relatives. "Then Laban said to Jacob, because you are my relative, should you therefore serve me for nothing? Tell me, what shall your wages be?" (Gen 29:15) He wants Rachel for payment. He will serve seven years and she will be his wife. He serves the seven years and Laban gives Jacob who he thought was Rachel to consummate the marriage. The woman turns out to be Leah, Laban's firstborn, and after they slept together (how he did not know, I have no idea) Jacob said, "What is this you have done to me? Was it not for Rachel that I served you? Why then have you deceived me?" (Gen 29:25). Notice the language, *"Why have you deceived me?"* Deceived. Jacob is getting some of what he has dished out to his brother and father. It doesn't feel good to be on the other side of deception. Sometimes the only way we "get" things in our life is when we feel what it feels like to be on the other end of what we ourselves are dishing out. So, Jacob gets Rachel a week later and then serves another seven years to pay for her.

Jacob is growing and prospering. He has eleven sons and multiple livestock and after two decades, is now in a place where he is ready to go home, back to his father Isaac and back to the land that God promised. Laban does not want him to go because he does not want to lose his daughters and grandchildren. He also understands that God has blessed him on account of Jacob. Jacob hears God tell him to go back, "Then the Lord said to Jacob, return to the land of your father's and to your family, and I will be with you" (Gen 31:3). Jacob starts organizing the troops. He calls Rachel and Leah and tells them that Laban has changed. He tells them about how he has served Laban and note this statement, "And you know that with all my might I have served your father. Yet your father has deceived me and changed my wages ten times, but God did not allow him to hurt me" (Gen 31:6-7).

Jacob is not the same person he was when he arrived at Laban's twenty years earlier. He has bore the brunt of deception and yet he acknowledges that God has been with him and that God has protected him. God speaks again assuring Jacob of his protection. "...for I have seen all that Laban is doing to you. I am the God of Bethel, where you anointed the pillar and where you made a vow to Me. Now arise, get out of this land, and return to the land of your family" (Gen 31:12-13). God is confirming that it is time to go back. Remember God said earlier that He would bring him back. Jacob said earlier that God would be his God if He gave him food and clothes and brought him back to the land in peace. He may be thinking, well, I have food and clothes but as far as peace, Esau still wants to kill me, Laban is mad, and I have got all this livestock—yeah, it's a blessing but they stink and I am tired of the constant noise. But God tells him to go. The daughters are concerned about their inheritance, "Is there still any portion or inheritance for us in our father's house?" (Gen 31:14-16). Since there is not they said, "Do whatever God has told you." In other words, there is no money for us because Laban is mad, so you may as well do what God says. It's human nature to look at the profit and make that a determining factor for staying or going. In this case the daughters are covering their bases economically.

Jacob moved toward the mountains of Gilead and three days after he left, Laban found out and set out after him. He caught up with him, but before he did he had a dream and God said to him, "Be careful that you speak to Jacob neither good nor bad" (Gen 31:24). It seems Laban is concerned about his "household gods," and he accuses Jacob of stealing them. "What have you done, that you have stolen away unknown to me, and carried away my daughters like captives taken with the sword...but why did you steal my gods?" (Gen 31:26-30). Now it was actually Rachel who took them, and when Laban came in to look for them in her tent she said, "The manner of women is with me" (Gen 31:35). That means it was her "time of the month", which scares Laban away.

Laban can't find anything and Jacob becomes angry. Notice in this statement how he summed up the last twenty years.

> "Then Jacob rebuked Laban, 'What is my trespass? What is my sin, that you have so hotly pursued me? Although you have searched all my things, what part of your household things have you found? Set it here before my brethren and your brethren that they may judge between us both! [He is really setting forth his case.] These twenty years I have been with you; your ewes and your female goats have not miscarried their young, and I have not eaten the rams of your flock. That which was torn by beasts I did not bring to you; I bore the loss of it. [That's pretty rich coming from a recovering deceiver.] You required it from my hand, whether stolen by day or stolen by night. There I was! In the day of the drought consumed me, and the frost by night, and my sleep departed from my eyes. Thus I have been in your house twenty years; I served you fourteen years for your two daughters, and six years for your flock, and you have changed my wages ten times. [Sounds like the United Auto Workers Union.] Unless the God of my father, the God of Abraham and the Fear of

Isaac, had been with me, surely now you
would have sent me away empty handed.
God has seen my affliction and the labor
of my hands, and rebuked you last night"
(Gen 31:36-42).

This brief statement sums up Jacobs life for the
last twenty years. He was doing all the right things
but Laban, his uncle, was being unfair, changing his
wages and, in today's vernacular, was "messing with
his head."

Wherever you are in your life right now, if you
love God, you're where God wants you. That doesn't
mean He wants you to stay there, there is a time to
leave. Leave a bad job, abusive marriage, or unhappy
circumstances. But before you run, pray and wait on
God and let Him set up your departure. Jacob was
faithful for twenty years, and did not leave until God
spoke to him to go back to the "land of his fathers."
God will speak to you too. Listen, if you hear nothing,
stay in your place, be faithful and continue to listen for
the still small voice.

I remember when I was driving a transit mix concrete truck; we would pull the truck under the plant to
receive the material. (Concrete is a mixture of sand,
stone, cement and water.) As the barrel spins on the
truck it mixes the material as it fills up. You can hear it
going in and you just wait, then you hear the vibration
of the bin, making sure that all the stone and sand is
out. When you hear that, you know it's not long be-

fore you hear the buzzer to tell you your drum is full and now it's time to back out. If you back out too early the material will end up on the ground. (And the boss will yell at you.) You have to wait until you hear the buzzer, then you move. Wait to hear the buzzer. I remember sometimes it would take a long time to get loaded, and I would get anxious and wonder, "What is the problem?" I would either get on the radio or go upstairs where they were loading the material. Many times it was trouble with material or mechanical problems. They said, "Just wait until you hear the buzzer." Okay, I will just wait. Waiting is hard work, especially when you're trusting the God of the universe. (He is totally on a different time schedule.) If God is with me and on my side, why the big wait? That's the tough part. Jacob waited twenty years, Jesus thirty, Moses forty.

After some more exchanges Laban finally left and went back to his house, "And early in the morning Laban arose, and kissed his sons and daughters and blessed them. Then Laban departed and returned to his place" (Gen 31:55). Finally the cord is cut between Laban and Jacob. Jacob is now free to go back in peace. Oh—that's the other part of the deal, "to bring me back in peace" (Gen 28:21).

Coming up is the good part. All the conflict of the last twenty years is going to pay off for Jacob spiritually.

"So Jacob went on his way and the angels of God met him. (He didn't see the angels on TV; they actually came to him—amazing!) When Jacob saw them he said, 'This is God's camp,' and he called the name of that place Mahanaim (Double Camp). Then Jacob sent messengers before him to Esau, his brother, in the land of Seir, the country of Edom (Gen 32:1-3).

Jacob sees angels, but he is still afraid of his brother. He wants to make amends; this is unfinished business. In the back of his mind for the last twenty years he's been thinking about his brother, what he did to him and how Esau wanted to kill him. Esau knew where he was so at any time he could have killed him, but he did not.

However, perception is reality, so when Jacob thought, "Esau is going to kill me," that's what motivated him to send gifts to appease his brothers wrath. After Jacob prayed he sent gifts,

"So he lodged there that same night, and took what came to his hand as a present for Esau his brother: two hundred female goats and twenty male goats, two hundred ewes and twenty rams, thirty milk camels with their colts, forty cows and ten bulls, twenty female donkeys and ten foals" (Gen 32:13-15).

(That seems excessive to me—but maybe back then that was considered normal.) Jacob told his servants to deliver them to Esau. With this he hoped that Esau would forgive and forget. "...I will appease him with the present that goes before me, and perhaps he will accept me" (Gen 32:22).

Again, these are not perfect circumstances to find God. Turmoil, fear, excessive burden of the past, this is where Jacob was in his circumstances. I remember when I became a Christian; it was not in a church service, with great music, perfect lighting and air conditioning. No one said to me, "Brother, do you want to go forward during the alter call? Do you want to pray the 'sinner's prayer'?" I was hearing music but it wasn't Third Day—or any other Christian groups for that matter. In fact, it was the sounds of the British group Yes, the southern sounds of Lynyrd Skynyrd, and two of Detroit's favorites, Ted Nugent and Bob Seger. (Bob is still one of my favorites; don't tell anyone.)

I was running from God and I knew it. "When He comes, (the Holy Spirit) He will convict (cause to see) sin, righteousness and judgment" (John 16:8). Through a number of circumstances I began to read the Bible, and what I read was not only enlightening but also disturbing. I began to understand that God was calling me and speaking to me to turn from my destructive behavior and let Him take hold of my life. The more I understood this the more my heart was resistant, until the experience I had at this particular concert. As I began to feel guilt about my choices and a sense that God was indeed calling me, I determined to "drown out" these feelings with any drug I could find. (There were a lot of them out there.) We had already taken blotter acid which was putting us in a different world. I was hallucinating and according to my friends I was on a "bad trip," but I knew it was more than that. I saw one of my neighbors with his back against the wall of Rich Stadium (where the Bills play) trying to get the last hit off a joint that looked like it burned out ten minutes earlier. I thought to myself, "I do not want to be like him," but in reality that is exactly where I was heading.

I heard a man say once, "The real you makes a demand on the you that you have become, or are becoming." That is what was going on with me. The real me—my soul, my inside man—was speaking to me, saying, "What are you doing? This lifestyle will not take you where you want to go." I literally thought that I was losing my mind and that I was going to stay on this bad trip forever. Dream world and true reality were merging into one. I knew the difference but could not bring myself out of where I was. Like Jacob, I was afraid.

Finally, we left the stadium and headed home. I woke up on a Sunday morning—gratefully the drugs had worn off and I was in my right mind. I knew I had unfinished business though, but I did not know if the transaction was going to go through. I wondered if God would forgive my antics and rebellion. I lay on my bed and this is what I said, "I don't know if You will forgive me, but if You will I will serve you the rest of my life," (or something like that). It is hard to explain, and I know the skeptic will question what happened to me next, but I felt an unexplainably deep peace. I knew that I was forgiven. God actually forgave me!

To the skeptic I will say, after thirty years — though I am not perfect — I still believe. Even after all the turmoil of the car crash that left me paralyzed, I still believe. I believe now, not only because of an experience, but because I am convinced that, after studying the Faith in Bible College and Seminary for many years, what the Bible says is true.

Then Jacob had a dramatic encounter with God. He has had a few, but this one is going to be life changing.

> "And he arose that night and took his two wives, his two female servants and his eleven sons, and crossed over the ford of the Jabbok. He took them, sent them over the brook, and sent over what he had. Then Jacob was left alone, and a Man wrestled with him until the breaking of the day. Now when He saw that He did not prevail against him, He touched the socket of his hip, and the socket of Jacob's hip was put out of joint as He wrestled with him. And the Man, [who many scholars call a 'Theophany', which is a God appearance — many believe Him to be the God Man, Christ Jesus] said, 'Let Me go, for the day breaks.' But Jacob said, 'I will not let you go unless you bless me!' So He said to

> him, 'What is your name?' He said, 'Jacob.'
> And God said, 'your name shall no lon-
> ger be called Jacob, (Deceiver) but Israel,
> (Prince with God) for you have struggled
> with God and with men and have pre-
> vailed'" (Gen 32:22-28).

Can you imagine God coming to you and changing your name? If you're a Christian that really is
what happened the moment you placed your faith in
Jesus. You are now pronounced the righteousness of
God in Christ (2 Cor 5:21). That is your new status.
So your encounter with God may not be as dramatic
as Jacob's, but it doesn't have to be. You are who God
says you are the moment you believe. Your struggle
is not in vain. You may have struggled with people
in bad circumstances, various jobs or social settings.
Your prayer life may be a struggle but you have kept
on praying. You, like Jacob, may have bore these con-
flicts for years. Jacob was rewarded with a fresh experience with God and this carried him. I believe you
can expect the same.

Esau had gotten over his anger and no longer wanted to kill Jacob. After a verbal exchange they agreed
to part ways as friends. "So Esau returned that day
on his way to Seir. And Jacob journeyed to Succoth"
(Gen 33:15-1). Jacob had lived for twenty years thinking that Esau wanted to kill him. Esau had long since
given up the whole thing, but Jacob had not gotten the
message. (No cell phones or instant messaging back

then.) We should keep short accounts with people, lest we become the ones who are negatively affected.

God told Jacob to go back to Bethel, "And God said to Jacob, arise, go up to Bethel, and dwell there; and make there an altar to God, who appeared to you when you fled from the face of Esau your brother" (Gen 35:1). Jacob told his family to put away strange gods, and they did. Now Jacob's faith is more solidified as he looks back on where he came from, his perspective is different; he sees the hand of God in all that he went through. "... I will make there an altar to God, who answered me in the day of my distress, and was with me in the way which I went" (Gen 35:3). As he looks back he can say with all his heart that God did exactly that.

This is different from his earlier encounter with God where he was basically bargaining, saying, "If you will do all these things and bring me back to this place, then you will be my God." Now looking back, he confirms that God really was with him. Sometimes it's only after we get through something and look back do we see the hand of God in it. While going through it we feel that God is nowhere to be found. Issues arise in our hearts that make us question God and His dealings. But when we hold on in faith and patience, looking back we may say, "Look what the Lord has done!" Sometimes in this life we get to see the hand of God in the here and now, as in Jacob's case. But sometimes we have to hold on until the end, with no answers, maybe still full of doubt on our death bed, holding on by the skin of our teeth, saying, "Lord I believe, help me with my unbelief." It is the struggle of the soul with the unseen.

My father-in-law was a man of faith. Though if you asked him about it he would not say that he was a man of God or of faith, Wally would say that he has been saved by Jesus Christ. He would not say that he was great in any sense of the word. I watched his body slowly deteriorate as a result of pancreatic cancer. I was in the room with him when he died, and I felt honored to be there. If you asked Wally if his life had any affect on people he would say, "Not much." Though he was always looking for opportunities to share his faith, he did not think he was making much of a difference. At his funeral, though he lived in a small town, the line for visitation was out the door. People I am sure he did not know very well, and probably would not consider "friends", were standing in a long line to say a final goodbye to this window washer, who, in some small way by his own amiable charm, affected them.

You do not know the affect you may have on other people's lives. Although you have not seen many of your dreams come true, if you really walk with God, then there will be a rich welcome in the Kingdom of God when you die. My father-in-law, I believe, is enjoying heaven in a strong way at this very moment— and I know he died with many questions and frustrations. But he died in faith. He had faith till the end, quoting a part of the verse from Colossians, "...Christ in me the hope of glory" (Col 1:27). Christ was in him, He was his hope till the end.

> God appears to Jacob again,
> "... when he came from Paddan-Aram and blessed him, and God said to him, 'Your name is Jacob; thy name shall not be called any more Jacob, but Israel shall be your name.' Also God said to him, 'I am God Almighty; be fruitful and multiply; a nation and a company of nations shall proceed from you, and kings shall come from your body. The land which I gave Abraham and Isaac I will give to you and to your descendants after you I will give this land'" (Gen 35:9-12).

If there is any doubt about whose land it is, if you believe God's word, this should clear it up. It is Israel's land, not the Arabs'. In regards to the land I want to share an insight. Earlier in Genesis we learn of the birth of two nations; the nation of Israel and the Ishmaelite nation. God is speaking to Sarah's servant Hagar after Abraham went to her and she conceived a baby. "And the angel of the Lord said to her: Behold, you are with child and you shall bear a son. You shall call his name Ishmael, because the Lord has heard your affliction" (Gen 16:11). But this was not the son of the promise. This is what God says about him, "He shall be a wild man; His hand shall be against every man, and every man's hand against him. And he shall dwell in the presence of his brethren" (Gen 16:12). The son of the promise, of course, was Abraham & Sarah's, Isaac. To this day this same conflict is still going on in the Arab nation which came out of Ishmael and has been at war with Israel from the beginning. Now with the Muslim religion and its Jihad, (Holy War) their hand is literally, "against every man." Just remember that God promised the land to Israel, the seed of Abraham, Isaac and Jacob.

Jacob was born to a chosen family. He was a twin who, by natural laws, should not have inherited the blessing of the first born. He got it by deception. Afraid for his life and under the direction of his mother, he flees his home. He joins with his uncle who himself is a deceiver. He lives with him for twenty years and his exterior life is prospering. He has two wives, eleven children and a bunch of animals. Finally, he gets the call from God to go back to his home. This is where he met God on his way out of town. It was here God spoke to him and promised to bring him back and give him the land. Under the stress of leaving Laban he meets God again. God speaks to him and changes his name from Jacob to Israel. He is no longer to see himself as Deceiver but rather a Prince with God. He wrestled with God and prevailed. Though his walk of faith started in turmoil, God still met him, gave him promises and followed through on all that He said He would do. Jacob learned and grew in his faith. He was not the same person after twenty years of being in the fire. He was made new and encountered God in a new way. You may have started your walk with God in less than ideal circumstances, and you may have been in a hard place for many years since. This does not mean that God has deserted you or that your faith is suspect. Hold on, "help is on the way," (as OnStar says) you're going to make it, just like Jacob did. From Jacob we will turn to the next person of faith—his son Joseph.

Chapter 2

A Dream, a Prison and a Head of State

In this story I see "Family Dynamics 101". Although it's not the main thing I want to focus on, it will come up, and we can gain insight from what happened to Joseph and his brothers. Joseph was a good kid, age seventeen when the story begins. His Dad loves him more than his other sons because he was the "son of his old age" (Gen 37:3). If I were counseling Jacob I would tell him, "Even though you feel this way about Joseph, don't show it. It will not be good for him or your other sons." And it wasn't. Jacob not only loved Joseph more, he actually gave him a multicolored coat that indicated that he was favored above the others. Dumb move. You may have more natural affection for one child over the other for many reasons. My advice is to be careful not to show it. Go above and beyond for the kid you have less affinity for. It will pay off in the end, and you will be the better because of it. (Too bad I was not around back then to give Jacob advice then all this would not have happened.)

His brothers did not like the fact that Jacob gave him the coat, and when Joseph had his dreams, they liked him even less, in fact—they hated him. "And Joseph dreamed a dream, and told it to his brothers and they hated him all the more" (Gen 37:5). Again, if I were counseling Joe I would tell him, "Watch who you tell what to." Sharing information with the wrong people could bring a great disaster to you. It's a huge temptation to tell everyone of a great blessing or a great problem. If you told of a great blessing the wrong people could "rain on your parade" at best, or worse—do you a lot of harm out of jealousy. If you tell your struggles to the wrong people they could judge you and make you feel worse than you already do.

Joseph is young and stupid; He tells. He dreamed two dreams and they both meant the same thing. The first is, "For behold, we were binding sheaves in the field, and lo, my sheaf arose, and also stood upright; and behold, your sheaves stood round about, and made obeisance to my sheaf" (Gen 37:7). The brothers got the point, "Shall you indeed reign over us" (Gen 37:8a). The next dream means the same, "...the sun and the moon and the eleven stars made obeisance to me" (Gen 37:9). He told this one to his father, "...Shall I and your mother indeed come to bow down... (Gen 37:10). The bothers hated Joseph all the more, but Jacob kept the matter in mind.

Apparently at one point, the brothers were away for more time than they should have been and Jacob was worried about them. He asked Joseph to go see if he could find out what was wrong and bring word back to him. Joseph left, as an obedient son to find his brothers, and ended up in Dothan where his brothers were. As soon as his brothers saw him they put a plan together, "Come now therefore and let us slay him and cast him into some pit, and we shall say, some evil beast has devoured him..." (Gen 37:20). After much debate they threw him into a pit, but when they saw the Ishmaelites, Judah said, "... come let us sell him to the Ishmaelites" (Gen 37:27). After they sold him they took the multicolored coat back to Jacob soaked in goat's blood. Jacob "tore his clothes and mourned many days" (Gen 37:34). This is how Joseph's faith walk began. Immaturity combined with God speaking to him, along with intense jealousy, were the ingredients that God was using to bring Joseph to his destiny and Israel to the next level of their survival and increase as a nation. As in Jacob's life, so with Joseph, these are unlikely circumstances for God to enter, but He does.

Joseph went from a young teenager living at home to being a slave in Egypt almost overnight. New places, new faces, he had to be wondering, "Where am I?" Here is one of the keys to seeing God's hand in this story. "And the Lord was with Joseph, and he was a prosperous man, and he was in the house of his master, the Egyptian" (Gen 39:2). That's really all you need to know; God is with you. If God is with you, you can rest; He is in charge.

It seems like Joseph was able to really trust God in this hard place. Everyone liked him and he had great favor with Potiphar, an officer of Pharaoh. Joseph may be thinking, "This isn't so bad; I am eating well; things are okay." And they were, until he is wrongly accused of trying to "hook up" with Potiphar's wife. Even without the Ten Commandments Joseph knew instinctively that it was wrong to sleep with someone's wife. When Potiphar's wife comes on to him he says, "There is none greater in this house than I; neither has he kept back anything from me but you, because you are his wife; how then can I do this great wickedness, and sin against God" (Gen 39:9). Amazingly, he even knew it was sin against God. Because the Law is written on our hearts, we know it.

She blows the whistle on him because she is scorned, and he ends up in prison. Again we have to remind ourselves that Joseph is human. He is subject to all the emotions of any man. Some people teach that he just joyfully jumped from phase to phase. I don't think so. In my case, after the crash that left me with no feeling or movement below my waist, I was distraught and heartbroken. In many ways I still am, but I chose (and it *is* a choice) to believe that God is God—that he is with me and for me, and that He will help me hold onto Him on this journey He's leading— no matter what.

When the disciples were confronted with the realties of what Jesus taught, many left; He turned to the twelve and asked, "Are you going also?" Their response was, "...Lord to whom shall we go? You have the words of eternal life. Also we have come to believe and know that You are the Christ, the Son of the living God" (John 6:66-69). This is faith. Not commanding material things to come into your life or speaking your problems away. No, it is holding on to the hand of

God in darkness, trusting Him to bring you out, and into His will for your life. Many say they trust God, and they do…but it is not until the rug is pulled out from under you and you have nothing but God, do you really know real trust. Trust in God. It's not always easy, but it is possible by His grace. This is what Joseph had to do—and did; trust God.

In prison Joseph prospered (Gen 39:23). Pharaoh was ruling as king in Egypt. Something happened and he was mad at two of his officers, the Baker and Butler, and threw them into prison with Joseph. They both dreamed dreams, and Joseph was able to interpret them. The Butler was going to be reinstalled in three days, and the Baker was going to die. The interpretation was accurate, "And he restored the chief butler unto his butler ship again and he gave the cup into Pharaoh's hand; but he hanged the chief baker; as Joseph had interpreted to them" (Gen 40:21-22). Joseph had a gift and a calling from God, and even though he was in prison, wrongly accused, inwardly broken, he was still able to use his gift for the benefit of others. After these supernatural events you would think that now he is going to get out of prison and be able to live his life normally—but he does not. "Yet the chief butler did not remember Joseph, but forgot him" (Gen 40:23). This went on for another two years. You may think it's your time for breakthrough / blessing / promotion, but it may be that you have to wait longer. When you don't know what to do, just pray and wait.

Then Pharaoh has a dream about seven fat cows eaten by seven sickly cows and seven good ears of corn eaten by seven thin ears. No one in his circle can interpret the dreams. Finally the butler remembers Joseph. A thought just came to me; there is no way the butler "forgot" Joseph. He may (and this is speculation), have been jealous of Joseph, thinking he would take his position or show him up somehow. Just a thought. Now though, it seems like there could be something in it for him. "Now I will tell Pharaoh about Joseph and maybe he will promote me or bless me in some way," he may be thinking. Anyway, the Butler told Pharaoh and Joseph was brought to him (Gen 41:9-14).

Joseph tells Pharaoh what the dream means.

"...the dreams of Pharaoh are one; God has shown Pharaoh what He is about to do: The seven good cows are seven years, and the seven good heads are seven years; the dreams are one. And the seven thin and ugly cows which came up after them are seven years, and the seven empty heads blighted by the east wind are seven years of famine. This is the thing which I have spoken to Pharaoh. God has shown Pharaoh what He is about to do. Indeed, seven years of great plenty will come throughout all the land of Egypt; but after them seven years of famine will arise, and all the plenty will be forgotten in the land of Egypt; and the famine will deplete the land. So

the plenty will not be known in the land
because of the famine following, for it will
be very severe" (Gen 41:25-31).

Almost instantly Joseph is made the head of
Egypt, second only to Pharaoh. "And Pharaoh said to
Joseph, inasmuch as God has shown you all this, there
is none so wise as you, you shall be over my house,
and according to your word shall all my people be
ruled: only in the throne shall I be greater than you"
(Gen 41:39-40). This man was born to lead. He led in
Potiphar's house, in prison and now in Egypt. Not all
of us are leaders like Joseph. I have heard some say
that Joseph was a special person with a special calling.
This is true. However, if you believe that God made
you, you have to believe He did it on purpose. You
have a purpose: maybe not to lead a nation, or even to
lead by your words—but what about influencing your
family or co-workers just by your example?

You may be in a hard place right this minute. Your
dreams may not be happening as you envisioned or
your heart is breaking over and over again. You wonder where God is and if your past experiences with
Him were even real. You wonder if you imagined
this God and His plan for your life, and think maybe
this is this some weird psychological mind game that
you played with yourself. Can you really trust God?
I think Joseph had those doubts too. He received the
dream as a young person, was abducted into captivity,
falsely accused, imprisoned and now set up as governor. "Joseph was thirty years old when he stood before

Pharaoh, King of Egypt. And Joseph went out from the presence of Pharaoh, and went throughout all the land of Egypt" (Gen 41:45). He had received the initial dream at seventeen, so from seventeen to thirty there was no fulfillment. Now at thirty, finally the dream is starting to come to pass, but it would take another seven years until his brothers would come and bow to him to fulfill his dream of thirteen years earlier.

Interestingly, Joseph was given a wife, Asenath, the daughter of Poti-Pherah (Gen 41:45). He had two sons by her who were born

> "...before the years of the famine came... the name of the firstborn Manasseh, (making forgetful), for God made me forget all my toil and all my father's house. And the name of the second he called Ephraim, (fruitfulness), for God has caused me to be fruitful in the land of my affliction" (Gen 41:50-52).

I think this shows the depth of his struggle. It wasn't just, "Oh well, praise the Lord." No, his pain went so deep that his kids bore its influence in their very names. In fact, he never did forget his father's house, but he was not controlled by the bad memories either. God was now prospering him and making him fruitful in the land of his affliction.

The dream came off as they had been told. Joseph did a wise thing; he stored up grain during the good years, knowing the famine was coming. Seven good years and now, "seven years of famine began to come, as Joseph had said" (Gen 41:54). The famine was great and it came about that, "... all the countries came to Joseph in Egypt to buy grain, because the famine was severe in all lands" (Gen 41:57). Jacob sent all his sons except Benjamin down to Egypt to buy grain from Joseph. When his brothers finally got to where he was they, "...bowed down before him with their faces to the earth" (Gen 41:6). Amazingly, Joseph did not act as you would think. He was no longer an immature boy gloating over a dream that made him look good. He did not say to his brothers, "see the dream happened just like I said, you bunch of losers." No, he was humble and broken by his experiences and reacts wisely. "Joseph saw his brothers and recognized them, but (when they didn't recognize him), he acted as a stranger to them and spoke roughly to them, 'Where do you come from?' And they said, 'From the land of Canaan to buy food' " (Gen 42:7-8).

Joseph's dreams from long ago came back to him. "Then Joseph remembered the dreams which he had dreamed about them" (Gen 42:9). It says, "*Then he remembered*," which makes you wonder, did he forget and now just remembered? In other words, he did not spend his thoughts wondering about when this dream would come to pass. Now that his brothers are before him, he remembers, "Oh yeah, this is what I dreamed about." It is hard to say for sure all that was going through his mind, but we know from scripture that he did dream and he did remember. He plans now what he is going to do. He accuses his brothers of being spies coming to, "...see the nakedness of the land"

(Gen 42:9). He tells them to bring back their youngest brother. "Send one of you, and let him bring your brother; and [the rest of] you shall be kept in prison, that your words may be tested to see whether there is any truth in you or else, by the life of Pharaoh, surely you are spies" (Gen 42:16).

He kept them in prison for three days then told them to leave one person in Egypt, go and take grain back to your land, and then bring the youngest back. It's funny how they reacted to this, "Then they said to one another, we are truly guilty concerning our brother [Joseph], for we saw the anguish of his soul when he pleaded with us, and we would not hear; therefore this distress has come upon us" (Gen 42:21).

We have all done things we are ashamed of; at least most of us are ashamed, anyway. The eastern religions teach Karma. Basically it means what goes around comes around. We have picked up on this thinking and thus we think that when something bad happens it is because we did something wrong, even if the wrong done was years before. I was speaking at a MADD meeting once and they ran a video about a young man who killed his best friend while driving drunk. The brother of the young man who had been killed was saying how he and his brother had done bad things when they were young, (he was older in the video) and thought they had gotten away with it, but they really hadn't because now his brother was dead. In other words, he thought all the bad things they did in the past had resulted in the brother's death. Admit it or not—this is human nature. In some ways things do come around; for example, in the legal arena. But in this case, though what Joseph's brothers did was wrong, it was working out for a great blessing for everyone. It seems when God is really involved, the bad, contrary to Karma, works for a great blessing.

Here again one of the brothers thinks their past is haunting them, "And Reuben answered them, saying, did not I speak to you, saying do not sin against the boy [Joseph], and you would not listen? Therefore behold his [Benjamin's] blood is now required from us" (Gen 42:22). This was not the case at all, God was orchestrating a great deliverance for all people and yet the brothers could not see it. All they could see was their sin and what they had done to "deserve" this punishment. Now, even though God brought good out of bad, we should never do evil so that good may happen. Sin is always wrong. However, because He knows we cannot be sinless, God uses sin for His own purposes. He will even use the Antichrist for His ultimate purpose. You must try to get over a guilty conscience and exercise your faith in the God who not only forgives but restores and actually brings good out of evil.

I have to be honest; I have suffered from a guilty conscience all my Christian life. It is amazing how we can come to Christ and be delivered from sin, feel forgiven, clean and free, but quickly fall back into the same guilt we used to have that controlled us before we were converted. Like the Galatians who wanted to go back under the Law after having been delivered from it. Paul dedicates a whole book to the subject—making many arguments to help the new believers see that they did not have to obey the Law but rather follow the Spirit. "Oh foolish Galatians! Who has bewitched you that you should not obey the truth before whose eyes Jesus Christ was clearly portrayed as crucified? This only I want to learn for you: Did you receive the Spirit by the works of the law or by the hearing of faith?" (Gal 3:1-2). It is difficult to unlearn and to relearn, to be "…transformed by the renewing of the mind" (Rom 12:2). But it is necessary to have this experience to go forward in this walk of faith. Joseph as a young person was able to receive the dream from God. Simple child-like faith is what God honored in him. This is what carried him the rest of his life even as he grew in wisdom and understanding. When all the old tapes play inside your head, you must turn them off and play the CD of a renewed mind. Out with the old and in with the new. God is for you not against you.

The brothers left Simeon with Joseph and went back to Canaan where Jacob and Benjamin were. They explained to Jacob that the governor had spoken roughly to them and accused them of being spies. They told him that they were to bring Benjamin back to Egypt with them to prove their innocence. When the brothers began to empty their sacks, however, they found the money that was supposed to have been payment for the grain in them. Jacob saw the money and probably thought they were lying. He said, "You have bereaved me: Joseph is no more, Simeon is no more, and you want to take Benjamin. All these things are against me...My son shall not go down with you" (Gen 42:35-38). This was his first response, but after awhile Jacob agreed to let the brothers take Benjamin. Time and no food were speaking to him. If he did not send Benjamin they would die of starvation anyway.

When they arrived in Egypt they bowed before Joseph, and when he saw Benjamin his heart was moved. "Then he lifted his eyes and saw his younger brother Benjamin, his mother's son, and said, 'Is this your younger brother of whom you spoke to me?' ...now his heart yearned for his brother" (Gen 43:29-30). Joseph threw a dinner party for everyone and told his steward to fill the brothers' sacks with food and each man's money. "Also put my cup, the silver cup, in the mouth of the sack of the youngest" (Gen 44:1-2). After they left Joseph told the steward to go after them, find the cup and bring them back. He found the cup in Benjamin's sack, and returned to the city where Joseph was. Joseph told them they could all go back home except Benjamin, who would have to stay and be Joseph's slave because the cup was found with him. Joseph is giving them a little taste of what he had gone through over the years. He had been falsely accused, put in prison, and made a slave. On a much smaller scale he is giving it to his brothers—and they are starting to get it. Judah said to Joseph, "...God has found out the iniquity of your servants; here we are, my lord's slaves both [ourselves and] he also with whom the cup was found" (Gen 44:16).

Again the brothers are plagued with guilt, and rightly so, but they are about to get the revelation of their lives. Judah pleads with Joseph to keep him instead of Benjamin. He says if they come back without him that,

> "it will happen, when I come to your servant my father, and the lad is not with us, since his life is bound up in the lad's life, it will happen, when he sees that the lad is not with us, that he will die...for how shall I go up to my father if the lad is not with me, lest perhaps I see the evil that would come to my father" (Gen 44:30-34).

Judah is willing to sacrifice his life for his brother's. He has grown as well from the time they all sold Joseph out. It seems that they all are deeply troubled and sorry for what they did to Joseph and that, in their minds, is the reason all this is happening. It is not what you did yesterday that matters; it is what you are doing today. You may pay a price for what you did yesterday, but be a man or woman after God's heart and hold on through the storm.

All this is leading up to Joseph's "great reveal." The brothers have struggled for a season; things were hard for them, a lot of misunderstanding and questions. It is all leading up to this point. "Then Joseph could not restrain himself before all those who stood by him, and he cried out, 'Make everyone go out from me!' So no one stood with him while Joseph made himself known to his brothers. And he wept aloud and the Egyptians heard it. Then Joseph said to his brothers, 'I am Joseph; does my father still live?'" (Gen 45:1-3). After years of not seeing Jacob—no contact for twenty years—the first thing he asks about is his dad; the father/son bond is so great it never leaves the mind. This is the same amount of time that Jacob had been gone from his father and homeland while living with his uncle. Sometimes kids give this air that they don't need or want their father, but deep down they really do.

The brothers' reaction to all this, "...his brothers could not answer him, for they were dismayed in his presence" (Gen 45:3). Here is the revelation,

> "And Joseph said to his brothers, 'Please come near to me.' So they came near, then he said, 'I am Joseph your brother, whom you sold into Egypt. But now, do not therefore be grieved or angry with yourselves because you sold me here; for God sent me before you to preserve life'" (Gen 45:5).

Not until this time could the brothers get any relief from the feeling that what they had done to Joseph years earlier was the cause for all this current upset in their lives. Now once they see him and hear his voice they were greatly distraught, but as they understood God's plan and Joseph's forgiveness they experienced a great relief from all the mental torment that had plagued them for years.

In John Piper and Justin Taylor's book, *Suffering and the Sovereignty of God*, they argue against the idea that we live in a random universe and that the things that happen around us and to us are for a purpose. Nothing is random, it is all ordered. Joseph seems to concur,

> "For these two years famine has been in the land, and there are still five years in which there will be neither plowing nor harvesting. And God sent me before you to preserve posterity for you in the earth, and to save your lives by a great deliverance. So now it was not you who sent me here but God; and He has made me a father to Pharaoh, and lord of all his house, and a ruler throughout all the land of Egypt" (Gen 45:5-8).

Joseph said to his brothers, *"It was not you who sent me here but God."* Some may argue that God was moving His purpose forward and that of course He will do dramatic things to be true to His promise of making Abraham's seed like the sand of the sea. Look at how He worked for Abraham in the last hour giving him Isaac. Look at Jacob's great encounter with God and supernatural dreams. No doubt God was going to move like that for them, but for me? I don't think so.

Those who take the position that things are random and there is no real reason for the pain and suffering in their lives never see the hand of God in any of their trials. If they have been falsely accused, "sold down the river" by friends or family, they would say, "Oh well, that is just the way it is." I have thought about this position and I find it quite hopeless. Paul says in Romans that, "...whatever things were written before were written for our learning, that we through the patience and comfort of the Scriptures might have hope" (Rom 15:4). In other words, we should learn from the text how God works and some of His ways so that, in our attempt to wait on Him, be used of Him, and ultimately glorify Him, we would not lose heart. Bad things came to Joseph, but out of his own mouth came the words, "God sent me." He admitted that this whole thing was ordained by God. Looking back and seeing the present, he is convinced that God was the mastermind behind this whole ordeal.

I make the argument throughout this book that your faith is made strong in the hard times, and that in these times you make a determination of who you are and what you believe. Can you imagine one of Joseph's friends in prison telling him to pray a certain prayer, recite a certain saying, command that prison doors be opened, blah, blah, blah? I have said before that I love the "Word of Faith" people; I see them as very sincere and count myself as one of them in many ways. But here is where we all need to learn and grow. God may heal and deliver you today—and He may not. Every day that He doesn't, however, has nothing to do with a lack of faith on your part. Just the opposite—holding on in the midst of hell on earth reveals a higher level of faith. Joseph held on in the bad times and now that he is in the good times he is all about helping people, especially his family, the very ones that sold him out.

> "Hurry and go up to my father, and say to him, 'thus says your son, Joseph: God has made me lord of all Egypt; come down to me, do not tarry. You shall dwell in the land of Goshen, and you shall be near to me, you and your children and your children's children, your flocks and your herds and all that you have. There I will provide for you'" (Gen 45:9-11).

Joseph wept, kissed his brother Benjamin and all the rest of his brothers. The brothers have to be chagrined but they talk to Joseph and probably think, "We don't understand all this but let's go with it, were blessed!" They have gone from thinking that all the negative stuff that was happening to them was because of what they did to Joseph years before to seeing Joseph before them now, declaring them innocent and that this was God's will. Many people can't seem to understand the love of God, myself included. How can God love sinners? The Bible says "But God demonstrates His love toward us, in that while we were still sinners, Christ died for us" (Rom 5:8). How is it that—when God is involved—the bad things we do can actually produce good? But this really is how God works. He takes our fallen nature and blatant sin and turns it to good when we trust Him.

When Jacob was told that Joseph was still alive and that he was Governor of Egypt, "...Jacob's heart stood still, because he did not believe them. But when they told him all the words which Joseph had said to them, and when he saw the carts which Joseph had sent to carry him, the spirit of Jacob their father revived" (Gen 45:26-27). I can't imagine losing one of my sons, (I have two) thinking he was lost forever, then finding out twenty-plus years later that he is alive. Not only alive, but that he is head of state, a "somebody" looking out for many, feeding many. It is a phenomenal picture of grace, love, self revelation and ultimately the moving forward of God's supreme purpose. Things in your life are not the way they appear. All the "stuff" that is going on is not the reality, the reality is what God is doing behind the scenes to move things in a favorable direction for everyone. The key is being the kind of person Joseph was in your present circumstances. Misunderstood? Confused? Set back? Be faithful where you are; believe that God is working, even though you don't understand. Paul said to the Philippians, "Therefore, my beloved, as you have always obeyed, not as in my presence only, but now much more in my absence, work out your own salvation with fear and trembling; for it is God who works in you both to will and to do for his good pleasure" (Phil 2:12-13). No matter where you are physically, emotionally, mentally or spiritually—this is the answer. Move forward like Joseph; be faithful where you are. You probably won't be head of a nation, but on the other side in the kingdom of heaven you will be totally blessed.

In these next two stories we are going to see a common theme running through them. God works in our lives and is bringing us through our problems to a better place. The New Testament tells us that we are to be "conformed to his image" (Rom 8:29). Character is to be formed in us, and a part of that character comes from faith and patience in the dream that we believe God has given to us. Many times our faith is the reason for our struggles. You don't struggle with fulfillment of a dream that you feel is from God if you don't believe in God or in His will for your life. When someone is introduced to Jesus, many times they are taught that God has a great plan for their life. We subconsciously believe that this means we are going to be great in the eyes of men. What we really need to ask God daily is, "What is Your plan for me today? What great blessing can I be today?" If we can live a God-planned day, then we can start looking at what God has put in our hearts for the future and move in that direction. God's plans aren't our plans, however. Even though we may never see our dream come to pass, if we're moving toward it and checking in with God daily—then maybe just the journey was God's great plan for your life. Just the journey—and you'd better believe it takes faith to keep moving.

Hebrews chapter eleven talks about men and women of faith, some were blessed and prospered some did not (Heb 11:30-40). If you make prosperity a blanket for everyone then what do you do with those who suffer and are believers? The only thing to say to them (and I have heard it said) is that their faith is sub par. "You're not there yet," they say, "but hold on you will get there." Which means you will get to a place of prosperity—not necessarily Christ-likeness. For sure, if we are in a bad place, we want to get out. If we are sick we want to get better, if we are in a hole we want to get out of it, or if we are broke we want money. The human mind is always looking for solutions; it is not content with accepting, without a fight, things that are not the way they are "supposed" to be. David was "a man after God's own heart." He became "King in Israel." He had wives and stuff, but there were many years that he was on the run from Saul, things were not right in his life, and God gave him a solution.

Chapter 3

Faith That Lost and Recovered All

After many years of running from Saul, (the King in Israel) David was weary, he said,

> "...now I shall perish some day by the hand of Saul. There is nothing better for me than that I should speedily escape to the land of the Philistines; and Saul will despair of me, to seek me anymore in any part of Israel. So I shall escape out of his hand" (1 Sam 27:1).

David is weary; he has been on the run from Saul for many years, he is reaching his breaking point. He makes a plan, right or wrong, and defects to the Philistines. As I just said, the human mind will make a plan to get out of a mess. Notice he says, "There is nothing better for me..." Think about it; when despair hits your life, you make a plan to get away from the cause of the pain. In reality there were many things he could have done, like keep trusting God to make a way where there is no way. But he is not thinking rationally, he is responding to his fear and discomfort.

He could have been the writer of the lyrics, "We got to get out of this place if it's the last thing we ever do," by The Animals. This was his mind set. To defect to the Philistines was one of the worst things he could ever do, but that is what he did. Think twice about the exit strategy you are considering, it may be the worst thing you can do. David takes his six hundred men and his two wives and goes to Achish, the King of Gath. Remember Goliath of Gath? This is the same place David slew Goliath, and that event is what ushered him into the public eye. His faith and solid aim caused him to kill Goliath. Most people know the story about Goliath, rah, rah, rah. But very few know about the story of his defection to the Philistine army.

The plan seemed to work at first. "And it was told to Saul that David had fled to Gath; so he sought him no more" (1 Sam 27:4). At David's request Achish gave David the city of Ziklag, "...therefore Ziklag has belonged to the kings of Judah to this day. Now the time that David dwelt in the country of the Philistines was one full year and four months" (1 Sam 27:6-7). David was a warrior, he did for the Philistines what he did for Israel. He went and attacked their enemies, who were the Geshurites, the Girzites, the Amalikites and the Pepsilites (not really, just seeing if you're with me). He would leave nothing alive when he attacked these places. When Achish asked him about his exploits he would say, "...against the southern area of Judah, or against the southern area of the Jerahmeelites, or against the southern area of the Kenites" (1 Sam 27:10). He gave Achish the impression that he was killing his own people so that he could find favor in his eyes. "So Achish believed David saying, 'He has made his people Israel utterly abhor him; therefore he will be my servant forever'" (1 Sam 27:11-12). This would be like the president of the U.S. going to Iraq, submitting to Iraqi authority and killing their enemies, the allies of the U.S. It is utterly absurd to think about, but this is about what it was like with a few exceptions. David's fear of Saul has brought him to this. Fear is a powerful emotion that if not kept in check will produce disastrous results. The fear of man is a snare (Prov 29:25). Some scholars say that David only gave the impression that he was killing his own people. We do not know for sure, but either way it was not a good situation.

The Philistines,

> "...gathered their armies together for war, to fight with Israel. And Achish said to David, you assuredly know that you will go out with me to battle, you and your men. So David said to Achish, surely you know what your servant can do. And Achish said to David, therefore I will make you one of my chief guardians forever" (1 Sam 28:1-2).

Achish wants David to go and fight against Israel. The exchange here is hard to read, David did not say, 'Yes let's go", rather the phrase, *"Surely you know what your servant can do."* This may have meant, "Of course I will go, you know what I can do," or a statement meant to change the direction of what was asked. Regardless, it seems that the lords of the Philistines are not supportive of David's involvement with their armies, especially when they intend to go up against Israel.

> "Then the princes of the Philistines said, 'What are these Hebrews doing here?' And Achish said to the princes of the Philistines, 'Is this not David, the servant of Saul king of Israel, who has been with me these days, or these years? And to this day I have found no fault in him since he defected to me.' But the princes of the Philistines were angry with him; so the princes of the Philistines said to him, 'Make this fellow return, that he may go back to the place which you have appointed for him, and do not let him go down with us to battle, lest in the battle he become our adversary. For with what could he reconcile himself to his master, if not with the heads of these men?'" (1 Sam 29:4-5).

The princes want him out, but Achish wants him in. They go back and forth for a while but the princes won out and David went back to the land of the Philistines. "So David and his men rose early to depart in the morning, to return to the land of the Philistines. And the Philistines went up to Jezreel" (1 Sam 29:11).

This is the background of what is about to happen to David and his men. To be so discouraged that you would actually fight against your own people is quite amazing. There have been people (maybe even you) who once walked with God and who loved the church; however, they have been hurt by someone or oppressed by a leader. To the point where they say in their heart, "This is not what I thought it would be; these people are not what they say." Thus they defect to the "other side" which could be the world system. Not only do they turn away from God, they turn against his kingdom and children. To calm their own fears, or to meet some need inside, they cry out against the church and its leaders. I have known people like this. (Just take a look at who's totally misusing the "separation of church and state" clause or making fun of Godly people who are in the public eye.) Let's be honest, if you have been a member of a church body for very long, (a couple of weeks—just kidding) you probably have run into people and leaders who make you scratch your head and wonder, "Are these people even Christians?" It is a real problem in all denominations. You may have been tempted to defect from the church and even criticize the church. This is what happened to David but on a greater scale. He was not just a soldier or a medic in the army. He was the leader, the "General", appointed by God Himself through the Prophet Samuel. David ran opposition against his people and seemed pretty comfortable in doing so until something dramatic happened in Ziklag, the city where all his people were.

> "Now it happened, when David and his men came to Ziklag on the third day, that

the Amalekites had invaded the South and Ziklag, attacked Ziklag and burned it with fire, and had taken captive the women and those who were there from small to great; they did not kill anyone, but carried them away and went their way. So David and his men came to the city, and there it was, burned with fire, and their wives, their sons, and their daughters had been taken captive. Then David and the people who were with him lifted up their voices and wept, until there was not more power to weep" (1 Sam 30:1-3).

Here is the picture; Ziklag has been destroyed and all the wives and children have been taken away. David and all his men are distraught; all that they loved and worked for is gone. The men are frustrated by this and begin in their minds to accuse David. The text indicates that by their actions they show that they have had a change of heart toward David. Instead of seeing it for what it was, a random attack, they blamed the leader for bringing them to this place in their lives. "Now David was greatly distressed, for the people spoke of stoning him because the soul of all the people was grieved, every man for his sons and daughters" (1 Sam 30:6). Stone the leader, yeah that's a good idea, that's what they should do. George W. Bush is taking some big time heat for the Iraq war. It doesn't matter what side you're on, the fact is that Americans are dying and, as a result, Bush is the one they are mad at.

David's men are mad at him; they see him as the problem, rather than the Amalikites. Bush believes that the terrorists are in the Middle East and we must have a presence over there to keep them in check. Bush, in my opinion, is not the problem—the terrorists are.

I find this next statement totally amazing. It seems like the last thing I would have power to do if I were speaking out against the people of God. Many times if we sin, it takes a long time to get to the point where we feel like we can approach God. God is forgiving and loving and desires to respond to a sincere cry for help or mercy, but after over a year of seemingly warring against his own people you would think that, for David, it would take a while to feel like he could appeal to the God of the universe who called him to fight for and protect the Hebrew people. This however, is not the case. Listen to what he does, "But David strengthened himself in the Lord his God" (1Sam 30:6). He encouraged himself, he spoke to himself, and he found God to strengthen him as he called to Him. I used to get angry at preachers for making it seem to easy to be forgiven. Just ask God to forgive you and He will. I think deep down I wanted it to be harder. I wanted people to pay more for their sin. Unlike myself, (but I am getting better at this), David does not see God that way. Sin is a real problem, but the good news is that God gave us a remedy, a way out, a way to be forgiven. Just like that. After David's departure to the Philistines and his attacks against his people, when the hard time came directly to him, he is able to find God and His strength.

Not only is he able to be strengthened, he is able to ask the Lord what he should do—and to actually hear Him tell him what to do. "So David inquired of the Lord saying, 'Shall I pursue this troop? Shall I overtake them?' And He answered him, 'Pursue, for you shall surely overtake them and without fail recover all'" (1 Sam 30:8). This is the awesome thing about God, He does what He will. "For the gifts and the calling of God are irrevocable" (Rom 11:29). He didn't say David, "You idiot, how could you defect to the Philistines? That is the dumbest thing you could ever do. I am going to show you my wrath, you are going to suffer great hardship and as result you will lose your family and the men with you will eventually kill you and you will end up in hell, you poor miserable soul. You should have done it My way, then you would not be in this place." Thank God He did not say this; His response is loving and kind. He saw David's heart, that deep down he was really a "man after His own heart" (1 Sam 13:14).

I am not advocating sin—that would not be wise. God does not want us to sin or to turn from Him or against Him. But one thing I have come to believe more and more, He understands us and our feelings and all the reasons we do what we do. He has called us and will be faithful to us, even when we are not faithful to him. "This is a faithful saying, for if we died with Him we shall live with Him, if we endure we shall also reign with Him, if we deny Him, He also will deny us. If we are faithless, He remains faithful, He cannot deny Himself" (1Tim 2:11-13). David was a chosen man of God, chosen by God. He was a man who was after the heart of God, but this did not make all his choices perfect. It is possible to have a pure heart and make wrong choices. It happens all the time. I would have hesitated to say or write this years ago, feeling afraid that people would see it as an opportunity to sin.

If you're looking at the human relationship to God as a system of works, hoping your good outweighs your bad, doing bad and then doing good to make it up, you will be disappointed when you come to judgment day. Many people do live by this standard, and they don't even realize they are, in fact rejecting Christ in doing so. Paul said, "...for if righteousness comes through the Law [works] then Christ died in vain" (Gal 2:21). We will all stand before God, and all the good works we've ever done won't matter one bit if we rejected His Son; "...all our righteous acts are like filthy rags" (Is 64:6). We must trust in what Jesus did for us, that by his ultimate sacrifice we may have the benefit of God's grace. It is out of gratefulness that we should do good and not evil. God is Holy and His call is for us to be and do the same. But He is also greatly merciful—and mindful that we are but dust. "As a father pities his children, so the Lord pities those who fear Him. For He knows our frame; He remembers that we are dust" (Ps 103:10). We should learn from our and other people's poor choices and yet keep our eyes on the God who is over all and above all.

David gets a solid word from God, "You are going to get back all that was taken from you. It is not going to just come out of the sky; you are going to have to go after it. Just do what you always do, be the warrior that you are and I will direct you." (Paraphrased) This is what David did, "But David pursued, he and four hundred men; for two hundred stayed behind, who were so weary that they could not cross over the Brook Besor" (1 Sam 30:10). He did what he always did, but this time there was a special purpose. He found an Egyptian along the road that the Amalikites had left for dead because he was sick. Now, the Amalikites really had no place special to go, other than to party and celebrate about the things they took. The discarded Egyptian agreed to bring David and his men to where the Amalikites were on one condition, that they would not kill him. People do stupid things when they only have themselves on their minds. The Amalikites kicked this man to the curb, never thinking that he would be the one who would lead to their demise. Never leave anyone behind. Even though they may appear to slow you down, they could be your greatest asset in the long run.

The Egyptian led them to where the Amalikites were,

> "And…there they were, spread out over all the land, eating and drinking and dancing, because of all the great spoil which they had taken from the land of the Philistines and from the land of Judah. Then David

attacked them from twilight until the eve-
ning of the next day. Not a man of them
escaped" (1 Sam 30:16-17).

David and his men fought against the Amalikites,
and seriously kicked the living daylights out of them.
This particular battle was different in that God had
promised David would recover all. Not everything
we do has divine direction on it. Many times we do
things for a long time because it is just what we do. We
work, take care of our family, save for the future, etc.
We may be praying for a breakthrough in many areas
of our life, and yet it is not forthcoming—and then all
of a sudden something is different, something changes. David ran from Saul for years, praying that God
would deliver him from this insane king. In hindsight
I'm sure David would say that he should have waited
to see what God would do before he defected to the
Philistines, but he didn't. I am so convinced that God
is gracious and does not really treat us as our sins deserve, but provides good solutions in the midst of our
poor decisions. I think David learned lessons running
from Saul that he could never learn in the classroom
or even in the field alone with God.

Here is the grace of God in action; God is faithful
to His word. He is "able to do exceedingly abundant-
ly above all we ask or think, according to the power
that works in us" (Eph 3:20). For David and his men
he sure did.

"So David recovered all that the Amalikites had carried away, and David res-

cued his two wives. And nothing of theirs was lacking, either small or great, sons or daughters, spoil or anything which they had taken from them, David recovered all" (1Sam 30:18-19).

Interestingly, after this event the…

"Philistines followed hard after Saul and his sons. And the Philistines killed Jonathan, Abinadab and Malchishua, Saul's sons. The battle became fierce against Saul. The archers hit him and severely wounded him. Then Saul said to his armor-bearer, 'Draw your sword, and thrust me through with it, lest these uncircumcised men come and thrust me through and abuse me.' But his armor-bearer would not, for he was greatly afraid. Therefore Saul took a sword and fell on it. And when his armor-bearer saw that Saul was dead, he fell on his sword and died with him" (1 Sam 31:2-6).

David defected from King Saul to the Philistines in fear of his life, served the king of the Philistines for a year and four months, temporarily lost all his and his men's families to the Amalikites, was threatened by his own men, heard God tell him it's going to be alright, attacked the Amalikites and got it all back, and now his arch enemy is dead. What a deal. I guess the message here is this; discouragement is a very real thing. We all get it from time to time. For many it may last for months or years, sometimes decades. But there will be a time that God will speak to you, "It is time to recover all." You may have run from God, questioned His existence, and wondered if He was even real. This is what you have to get from David's story; no matter where you have run, it is time to strengthen yourself in the Lord your God.

Stand before Him in faith and refuse to believe all the lies that are in your own mind. I have found that the devil never stops speaking; he is the accuser of the brethren.

> "So the great dragon was cast out, that serpent of old, called the Devil and Satan, who deceives the whole world; he was cast to the earth, and his angels were cast out with him. Then I heard a loud voice in heaven saying, 'Now salvation and strength and the kingdom of our God and the power of His Christ have come, for the accuser of our brethren, who accused them before our God day and night, has been cast down'" (Rev 12:9-10).

He stands day and night speaking out against you and all you are doing or intend to do. In addition to this, your own logic and mental processes will hold you in a state of stagnation. In the midst of it though, God speaks, "You will certainly recover all." You are encouraged to "stand in faith, trust in God, lean not to your own understanding, in all your ways acknowledge Him" (Prov 3:5-6). This is what David did. He refused to be discouraged; he did not give up.

David honored authority, he did not retaliate against Saul who was still technically the king in Israel, although rejected by God, he was allowed to keep his place until God would remove him. It was not for anyone else to remove the king, but God. Though naturally, most would have (and did) tell David to try to defeat Saul any way possible. David waited for God to come through. Again, this is one of the most difficult things to do as a faith person, wait for God to act. We want to act now, and feel when we don't act we are not moving the way we should. There is a time to act and a time to wait, it's hard to figure out when to do what, but God will let you know. There are many great lessons in this story. Take what applies to you at this moment; the other lessons are for a different time. One thing is for certain though; true faith is based on God and His will and purpose, and is not about commanding things around. It is about trusting God in the furnace of trial and affliction, weather you or someone else brought it into your life. David brought a lot of hell into his own life but God never left him—He will never leave you either.

Chapter 4

Job and Real Faith

The last person I want to talk about to tie this all together is a great man of faith—Job. The one man I want to meet when I get to heaven is Job. I will walk past everyone else to get to him. In many ways, though I do not know him personally, I have, through his story, come to know him in such a way that I stand in awe of him. He is one of my heroes, right up there with Jesus, Paul and Brett Farve. (Joke) I can't wait to meet him personally. "There was a man in the land of Uz, whose name was Job; and that man was blameless and upright, and one who feared God and shunned evil" (Job 1:1). This was what God said about Job from the start, God pronounced him blameless and upright. We have to establish this right off the bat or confusion will settle around us and we will end up like Job's friends questioning his righteousness and his stand with God. If we are going to hit the bull's-eye in interpretation, our aim has to be right; and this pronouncement of his righteousness is pivotal in getting it right.

Job was a man of faith and love, and as a good father he was concerned about his kids.

"So it was, when the days of [his grown children's] feasting [partying] had run their course, that Job would send and sanctify them, and would rise up early in the morning and offer burnt offerings according to the number of them all. For Job said, 'It may be that my sons have sinned and cursed God in their hearts.' Thus Job did regularly" (Job 1:5).

This was something that was a part of Job's life. He was fearful that his kids were not living right. Most parents, no matter what their religious background, are concerned that their kids are doing right, making the right decisions and really have the right inner life as well as the exterior life. Job was concerned that his sons may have, "cursed God in their hearts." He was thinking about their inner life, their true character. We all have both, an outer life we show to the world: our personality, our intellect and looks. Everyone sees the outer life before they see the inner—though the inner life many times shines through the outer. Job's outer life was just about perfect, he had health and wealth and was well respected in the community. It is his inner life that will be challenged by loss in his exterior life. This is our challenge as well.

This is really all we have in terms of background about Job. You can read commentaries about the book that may be helpful, but from a basic reading, this is what we have. Job was righteous and loved and prayed for his kids. This next section is about a behind-the-scenes look at what was going on in heaven while Job was on earth. I find this to be quite insightful as we try to figure out all that happened to Job and why.

> "Now there was a day when the sons of God [angels] came to present themselves before the Lord, and Satan also came among them. And the Lord said to Satan, 'From where do you come?' So Satan answered the Lord and said, 'From going to and fro on the earth, and from walking back and forth on it'" (Job 1:6-7).

There are only bits and pieces of who Satan is and where he came from in the Bible, here is one of them.

> "You were the anointed cherub that covers; I established you; you were on the holy mountain of God. You walked back and forth in the midst of the fiery stones. You were perfect in all your ways from the day you were created. Till iniquity was found in you" (Ez 28:14-15).

It seems that Satan, or Lucifer, was a Cherub, which is the highest order of spirit beings, established by God and was perfect. As a free moral agent Lucifer himself was able to choose wrong. God did not create iniquity; it was found in him. He chose to rise up against God. Here is another passage that describes Satan and his anarchy against God.

"How you are fallen from heaven, O Lucifer, son of the morning! How you are cut down to the ground, you who weaken the nations! For you have said in your heart: I will ascend into heaven, I will exalt my throne above the stars of God; I will also sit on the mount of the congregation on the farthest sides of the north; I will ascend above the heights of the clouds, I will be like the Most High. Yet you shall be brought down to Sheol, to the depths of the Pit" (Is 14:12-15).

So this is the same entity that was approaching God in relation to Job. In this case the Devil was present when the sons of God [angels] came to pray. Interestingly, it is the Lord who takes the initiative in asking Satan about Job, "Then the Lord said to Satan, have you considered my servant Job, that there is none like him on the earth, a blameless and upright man, one who fears God and shuns evil" (Job 1:8). This book has produced a lot of controversy; many people have tried to figure out how to interpret the book of Job. This is what the text plainly says, *"the Lord said to Satan."* This does not mean that Satan wasn't thinking about it already. "Oh no, I have never thought about destroying Job." That is what he is all about: stealing, killing and destroying. "The thief does not come except to steal, and to kill and to destroy" (John 10:10). But in this case it is God Himself who seems to be the one behind this trial and will use Satan for

His purposes. It seems that sickness, pain and death are not from God directly. They come from the fall of man in the garden and the Devil; however in God's massive wisdom and overwhelming understanding He permits and uses them for His purpose. We are going to see this more and more in Job's life.

> "So Satan answered the Lord and said, 'Does Job fear God for nothing? Have you not made a hedge around him, around his household, and around all that he has on every side? You have blessed the work of his hands, and his possessions have in-creased in the land'" (Job 1:9-10).

Satan accuses God of coddling Job and setting him up so that he would naturally serve God with total de-votion because of God's blessings and protection. This also shows that God is the One who makes things in-crease. He is behind the prosperity of all men. Even when the wicked prosper they are storing it up for the righteous (Ecc 2:26b). Satan taunts God, "But now stretch out your hand and touch all that he has, and he will surely curse you to your face!" (Job 1:11). I have often wondered why God would respond to Sa-tan like He does. He could have handled this in so many different ways, like saying, "Buzz off Devil, I don't like you and I am stronger than you; you're the bad guy", but He didn't. "And the Lord said to Satan, 'Behold all that he has is in your power, only do not lay a hand on his person.' So Satan went out from the presence of the Lord" (Job 1:12). God says, "Okay, do whatever you want to his stuff, including his sons and daughters—but do not touch him."

The next section deals with all that Satan did to Job's family. The Sabeans raided the fields where servants were tending his donkeys and oxen; they took the livestock away and killed the field servants. Fire came down and burned and killed all the sheep, the camels and the farm servants. Then Satan attacked Job's family. A great wind came and destroyed the house of one of the sons and killed all his sons and daughters who were in it (Job 1:13-19). The devastation was great—beyond comprehension. I said in my book, *Walking This Walk*, that when we read about something, we only gain understanding of it on one level. It is so easy to read what happened but not feel the full effects. Truly we can only imagine what this was like. Katrina happened a few years ago; at first we were all upset at the devastation, and maybe a few of us actually did something about it. For most of us though it was soon "out of sight out of mind." We become detached from the reality of people's pain. I never fully understood spinal cord injury or the wheelchair life, and what I did understand I only did superficially. Now I have personal experience, therefore my understanding is much deeper. Job loved his family; he prayed for them daily. He was concerned for their hearts and now they are all gone—in an instant.

We have to remember that there was no book of Job for Job to read and try to determine how he should respond to this event. We do not know for sure what or how much of the Scriptures he actually had. It may have been enough though for him to have understood the character of God in a real way; that God is loving and kind even though circumstances don't always seem so. In any case, this is how he responds,

> "Then Job arose, tore his robe, and shaved his head; and he fell to the ground and worshiped. And he said, naked I came from my mother's womb, and naked shall I return there. The Lord gave and the Lord has taken away; blessed be the name of the Lord. In all this Job did not sin nor charge God with wrong" (Job 1:20-22).

Maybe if he knew what was going on behind the scenes he would have charged God with wrong. "God, how could you allow this to happen? Why would you even give the devil the time of day much less give him permission to do all this?" This, I have seen, is the heart's war against God. I have heard young people say, "Life is just a cruel joke that God is playing on us, I cannot serve a God who is like this." I have to say, it is a hard pill to swallow, and I do not write this lightly. Suffering is hard. No matter where it comes from; it is not easy. This is what disturbs me about some preaching I have heard, which gives the impression that God is the great Santa Claus in the sky, and that if you really believe Him your life will be without suffering and he will give you whatever you ask. This is not biblically accurate and we are going to see that God has His reasons for doing what He is doing. One of the reasons is for us and our benefit—really. My hope is that by the end of the book we are going to see God differently, in a very positive way, like Job did.

I find his first response to the tragedy that hit him amazing. For most people this would not be their initial response. Maybe after a while (especially if they read the book of Job and figure out how they're supposed to respond) they may come to this point, but as a first response—I don't think so. For Job, as the book plays out, his "friends" are going to bring out another side of his struggle, but for now he is right on. God gives and God takes away. I heard a preacher say, "God gives and never takes away," in other words, God is not an "Indian Giver"; He will not require back that which He gave. For the most part this is true, but He still holds the keys to whatever He chooses to do. "...Our God is in heaven; He does whatever He pleases" (Ps 115:3). It is quite shallow and could be materialistic to say that God would never take back what He initially gave. The story of Job reveals that this is not true. More on that later.

Job Part Two begins to play out as the devil comes before God again. "And the Lord said to Satan, 'From where do you come?' So Satan answered the Lord and said, 'From going to and fro on the earth, and from walking back and forth on it'" (Job 2:2). He is in the same place; he is not too creative. He just wanders—actually Peter says he, prowls. "Be sober, be vigilant; because your adversary the devil walks about like a roaring lion, seeking whom he may devour" (1 Peter 5:8). He is a defector, a distorter of heaven, a rebel

against God and all truth. God and Satan are dia-
metrically opposed to each other in their motivation
toward the human family. The truth though, is that
God is not moved or mocked; He uses Satan for His
own purposes. I remember watching *Raiders of the
Lost Ark* one day. In one scene this man is wielding a
machete toward the main character, Indiana Jones. He
is a good distance away and yet seems quite threatening, doing all these fancy moves with the long knife
over his head. Indiana pulls out a gun and shoots
him—just like that. I think this is a good mental picture of this conflict. Though the Devil is allowed to
seemingly run roughshod over the human family and
seems ominous in his threats, God is still in control. (I
know it doesn't seem like it with all the devastation,
but hold on, let's keep going through this book.)

The Lord said the same thing to him as He did before, "Have you considered my servant Job?" (Job 2:3).
This is where it gets crazy, the devil says, "...skin for
skin! Yes all that a man has he will give for his life. But
stretch out Your hand now, and touch his bone and his
flesh, and he will surely curse You to Your face!" (Job
2:4-5). This is the same scenario as the first encounter;
God seems to be the one starting it, "*have you considered my servant Job?*" Satan is not all-knowing; he as-
sumes that Job will curse God if he is allowed to crush
his body. I don't think we should disregard Satan, or
play around with him, but we need to understand
what scripture says about him. Scripture says to fear
God and keep His commandments; we should rever-
ence God above Satan. God responds to Satan,

"Behold, he is in your hand, but spare his life. So Satan went out from the presence of the Lord, and struck Job with painful boils from the sole of his foot to the crown of his head. And he took a pot shard with which to scrape himself while he sat in the midst of the ashes" (Job 2:6-8).

This is the picture; a man with painful boils—not just boils, but *painful* boils—sitting in ashes scraping the boils with broken pottery.

I have known pain since I was crushed by a drunk driver several years ago. Many ribs and vertebra were broken, and from the time of the crash I have had fiery nerve pain in my legs and a terrible stabbing pain in my low back. I have called out to God for relief. In addition to all of the standard treatments, I also went to the Miami Project in Miami, Florida in August of 2007 to have a de-tethering surgery, where they go into the spinal cord and remove scar tissue and bone fragments in hopes that this will relieve pain. I am hopeful that the pain will recede in time.

Job sat in great pain. He lost his family and now his health is fading away. Listen to what his wife says, "...do you still hold on to your integrity? Curse God and die!" (Job 2:9). Wow, what a vote of confidence. I'm sure part of him wanted to do just that. We will see later that he talked about wanting to die, but the one thing he will not do is curse God. He will not let go of the truth that God is good despite what he is going through. "But he said to her, you speak as a foolish woman speaks. Shall we indeed accept good from God and shall we not accept adversity? In all this Job did not sin with his lips" (Job 2:10).

I find this quite astounding that while atheists and skeptics can go on and on about all the "bad" things in life, many times they don't address the good things in life. Where did all the good come from? Very few people have had all bad and no good. Possibly some who grow up in war torn areas, with poverty and disease, but for the most part, most people have known and received some good in life. The glory of the sun rising or setting is a beautiful thing that anyone who has general health and well being can appreciate. "The heavens declare the glory of God the earth shows the work of His hands" (Ps 19:1). Job understands that good and bad—or as he says "adversity", which is really, uh…bad—comes from God. Some say evil does not come from God. They say that the bad comes from Satan who controls bad people. Part of this is true, as we saw in the beginning; Satan is allowed to afflict Job. He is behind tragedy and problems no doubt. But another question to ask is who controls Satan? The answer: God does. If God had no reins on him, I think we would not be here; Satan would have destroyed us all by now. If the devil is the one behind all the mayhem in the human family, where does that leave God? So if we accept that the devil is the one who brings the destruction without regard for God and His power and wisdom, I think we err. God is in charge—not him. That is why we "count it all joy when you fall into various trials, knowing that the testing of your [personal] faith produces patience" (James 1:1-2). I think we can say all trials are monitored for each individual person and every "bad" thing comes to them because a sovereign God thinks it is right to do so and knows it will work out for good in the end. Job's understanding is reflected in his response, which must have been correct because it says that Job did not sin with his lips. He did not curse God, nor did he speak wrongly of Him.

For further insight, Matthew has some good information about Satan and God, in this case God in the flesh, Jesus of Nazareth. This is quite amazing and insightful: "Then Jesus was led up by the Spirit into the wilderness to be tempted by the devil. And when He had fasted forty days and forty nights, afterward he was hungry" (Matt 4:1-2). The scene is set. Jesus had fasted, was hungry, and then the Spirit led him to a place where he would be tempted by Satan. In our minds we wonder why the Spirit would set him up like that. That is the last place we would think that anyone should go, much less the Son of Man after fasting all that time. What a cruel thing to do, we think. But this is what happened, and God has a reason for everything.

This is Satan's first temptation, "'...if You are the Son of God, command that these stones become bread.' But he answered and said, 'It is written, man does not live by bread alone but by every word that proceeds out of the mouth of God'" (Matt 4:3-4). The temptation and the rebuttal. Notice Satan said, "*...if*

You are the son of God." He wanted Christ to doubt who He was and then wanted Him to use His power to do something that was against the will of God. But Jesus was not going to enter into the trap that the devil was setting. We are going to see how Job was also tempted to doubt his place before God. This is a great ploy of Satan to get us to doubt who we are in Christ; He is our righteousness and He makes us right with God.

Here is the next scene.
> "Then the devil took Him up into the holy city, set Him on the pinnacle of the temple, and said to Him, 'If You are the Son of God throw yourself down, for it is written, He shall give His angels charge over you, and, in their hands they shall bear you up, lest you dash your foot against a stone.' Jesus said to him, 'It is written again, you shall not tempt the Lord your God'" (Matt 4:5-7).

The devil taunts him again, "If you are the Son of God..." and this time he uses Jesus' own weapon—scripture. "It is written ...he shall give his angels charge...", in other words, if you jump off this peak, God will save You. Jesus knew the scripture better than he did, and could actually quote it its proper context, which He did. (Back at you Satan—and make it a double.) As we continue in the book of Job we are going to see some similarities between how Job's friends spoke to him and how Satan is speaking to Jesus.

They took scripture out of context to condemn Job just like Satan misquoted scripture to tempt Jesus. Jesus' rebuttal was to aptly quote it in the correct context to push the enemy back. A man once said, "Truth not rightly divided in the pulpit, [or anywhere else] will bring bondage in the pew." This is a true statement. Here is the final attempt to get Jesus to give in.

> "Again, the devil took Him up on an exceedingly high mountain and showed Him all the kingdoms of the world and their glory. And he said to Him, 'All these things I will give to You if you will fall down and worship me.' Then Jesus said to him, 'Away with you Satan! For it is written, you shall worship the Lord your God and Him only you shall serve.' Then the devil left Him and behold, angels came and ministered to Him" (Mt 4:7-11).

Compare this to the encounter to the one in the book of Job. The Lord started the conflict in the book of Job, and the setting was heaven. The Matthew encounter was on earth, the Spirit did lead Jesus out to the wilderness to be tempted, so from that standpoint you could say that God initiated this as well. For sure God the Father, Son and Holy Spirit were active in this conflict, but Jesus did not give in. He was tempted in all areas of weakness (hunger, pride and greed) just like we are—yet he didn't give in to any of them. "For we do not have a high priest who cannot sympathize with our weaknesses, but was in all points tempted as we are, yet with out sin" (Heb 4:15). God knew that Jesus needed to go through this for our sake. The reason I'm bringing this into the mix is to show another dimension of Spiritual battle. No doubt the battle still rages today. The devil was behind Job's suffering and pain, though Job himself did not see this. Jesus saw this and He used the weapon of God's word to defeat Satan. We should do likewise.

When my kids were small we had a dog named Jake. Jake was a border collie who liked to run…away. Any chance he would get to bolt he would. We lived in a very populated area at the time, so we would have to keep him on a leash. Occasionally he would get loose and run through the neighborhood, but no car ever hit him. We moved out into the country, and one day Jake was run over by a propane truck. Naturally, you would think that his chances of survival would be greater in a less populated area, but he was still running wild and he paid the ultimate price.

We got another dog, Frankie, to take his place. Frankie is the opposite of Jake. She is obedient and does what we tell her to do. She loves to run after the ball, catch it, bring it back and want you to throw it so she can catch it again. I bought a lacrosse stick and threw the ball to her for long periods of time. We got another dog, Alice. (The dogs were my wife's idea, I like dogs—but she *loves* them.) Alice is a fox terrier and, because Frankie is a border collie, she would herd Alice into the corner for hours. Alice had wandering ways like Jake, and would run away if you didn't chain him up. (Or her, rather, but we named her after Alice Cooper—a blast from the past—so there was always kind of a gender conflict!) So that's what we did, chained him/her in the front yard, the same area where I would throw the ball to Frankie. Alice wasn't the crispest cracker in the box, so when the ball was thrown she would run after it along with Frankie. Problem—she was chained and could only go so far and when she reached the end, the chain would snap tight and her rear end would go flying in the air. She didn't get the concept so she would do it again and again. Quite funny!

The point to all this is that Satan is on a leash and God holds the retractor. He can go only so far and that's it. I am saying this from an overall perspective, not personal. People can allow Satan into their lives through many ways. In Jesus' day people were possessed by demons; and the same thing happens today—it's just that the world wants to find another explanation, so demon possession is not widely believed. How and why they come into people is a matter for another book. But according to the books of Job and Matthew, Satan is one being that has access to heaven and earth, talks to God, has a mission to tempt and destroy people, but was not created in the likeness of God. God's greatest creation, humans, he wants to destroy, but as Martin Luther said, "Satan is the ape of God." God is in charge—not him. I realize I've already said this, but repetition is not a bad thing, especially when it comes to this subject. You must get this for you to move forward in understanding. The hard times that have come into your life have a design; it is hand crafted by God Himself, (providing you did not, through poor behavior, bring it on yourself...but even if you did, when you turn it over to God, He will make a way back to Himself.) Many have done things they are later ashamed of, but found hope and restoration in God.

Jesus lived for thirty years as a hard-working carpenter with his father (as far as we know). Then on God's appointed day, Jesus was baptized by John the Baptist and his whole career changed.

> "When He had been baptized, Jesus came immediately from the water, and behold, the heavens were opened to Him and He saw the Spirit of God descending like a dove and alighting upon Him, and suddenly a voice came from heaven saying, this is My beloved Son, in whom I am well pleased" (Matt 3:16-17).

This dramatic event happened right before He was led out to the wilderness to be tempted. This temptation was the strategic kick-off to his debut as the Messiah. You may say, "That was Jesus, of course His life was going to be directed supernaturally," but if you ask about me, I don't think so. But the truth is that God loves you as much as He loves Jesus. His love is not compartmentalized, it is pure for all—and He will supernaturally orchestrate your life too.

That is why James said, (I'm repeating this scripture to support my point and to help you remember it,)

> "My brethren, count it all joy when you fall
> into various trials, knowing that the test-
> ing of your faith produces patience [endur-
> ance, perseverance]. But let patience have
> its perfect work, that you may be perfect,
> [mature] and complete, lacking nothing"
> (James 1:2-4).

Here it is, all our various trials may seem random, with no real value or purpose, but they are not. The reason for the trials is to produce a perfected faith; a faith that recognizes the real God—not the Disney God that much of America preaches. This Disney God gives you great things all the time and, if you give to Him, He will reward you one hundred times over. Is there a reward for faith? Yes, the reward for true faith is God Himself, not toys. This is where Job was headed, toward a great revelation that he hadn't had before. But there is going to be some bumps along the way in the form of "friends".

Chapter 5

Faith and "Friends"

"Now when Job's three friends heard of all this adversity that had come upon him, each one came from his own place—Eliphaz the Temanite, Bildad the Shuhite, and Zophar the Naamathite. For they had made an appointment together to come and mourn with him, and to comfort him. And when they raised their eyes from afar, and did not recognize him, they lifted their voices and wept; and each one tore his robe and sprinkled dust on his head toward heaven. So they sat down with him on the ground seven days and seven nights, and no one spoke a word to him, for they saw that his grief was very great" (Job 2:11-13).

These guys appeared to be broken over Job and all the hell that had hit his life. They made a determined effort to come to him, outwardly shared his grief in the custom of the day, and stayed right there in the ashes with him in silence because they saw that he was broken inside and out. They should have kept it that way and just not said anything. But, like most of us, they could not stay shut up but had to throw their two cents in, which is going to make it harder rather than easier on Job. One of the lessons the book of Job teaches is to know when to talk to a person who is suffering—and when to just listen and mourn.

After seven days and nights in silence Job starts to talk. "May the day perish on which I was born. And the night in which it was said, 'A male child is born.' May that day be darkness; may God above not seek it; nor may light shine on it" (Job 3:3-4). Job is suicidal. What happened to, "Naked I came and naked I will return, praise God" (paraphrased)? What is happening to Job is very human. When hard times come our first reaction may be right, "God has a reason for this," we righteously say. But as time passes and the hardness and reality of the trial sets in, we tend to speak out of our pain, which is what Job was doing at this point. This was not a theological response but a response based on pure and naked reality and pain. Pain is not easy to live with whether physical or emotional. Many times it is relentless in it mission to make us depressed and ineffective. It settles in for the long haul and attempts to form us into totally broken people beyond repair. I have known both physical and mental or emotional pain. I believe that physical pain is worse, in that we don't process emotional pain when we have intense physical pain. If we are free from physical pain it is then we can begin to process emotional pain. If someone is stabbing you in the back or hitting you with a bat, you're not going to be thinking about how your childhood abuse has affected you. It is just not going to happen. A hungry man is interested in one thing, food—that's it. Job has both types of pain and is crying out to his friends and wants comfort. It is not going to come though. After all Job's rant about wanting to die Eliphaz is the first to speak up and offer advice.

A popular book called, *When Bad Things Happen to Good People* written by Harold Kushner has been a source of comfort and encouragement to many. In it he writes in reference to Job and his friends.

> "Job's comforters genuinely wanted to cheer him up and help him recover from his losses and illnesses. But they did almost everything wrong, and ended up by making him feel worse. We should learn from their mistakes what a person needs when he has been hurt by life, and how we as friends and neighbors can be helpful to him. Their first mistake was to think that when Job said, 'Why is God doing this to me?' he was asking a question, and that they would be helping him by answering his question, by explaining why God was doing it. In reality, Job's words were not a theological question at all, but a cry of pain. There should have been an exclamation point after those words, not a question mark. What Job needed from his friends, what he was really asking for when he said,

'Why is God doing this to me?' was not theology, but sympathy. He did not really want them to explain God to him, and he certainly did not want them to show where his theology was faulty. He wanted them to tell him that he was in fact a good person, and that the things that were happening to him were tragic and unfair. But the friends got so bogged down talking about God that they almost forgot about Job—except to tell him that he must have done something pretty awful to deserve this fate at the hands of a righteous God. Because the friends had never been in Job's position, they could not realize how unhelpful, how offensive it was for them to judge Job, telling him he should not cry and complain so much. Even if they themselves had experienced similar losses, they would still have no right to sit in judgment of Job's grief. It's hard to know what to say to a person who has been struck by tragedy, but it is easier to know what not to say. Anything critical of the mourner, 'Don't take it so hard,' or 'Try to hold back the tears; you're upsetting people,' is wrong. Anything which tries to minimize the mourner's pain, 'It's probably for the best, it could be a lot worse, she is better off now,' is likely to be misguided and unappreciated. Anything which asks the mourner to disguise or reject his feelings, "We have no right to question God, God must love you to have selected you for this burden," is wrong as well".

He continues,

"Under the impact of his multiple tragedies, Job was trying desperately to hold on to his self respect, his sense of himself as a good person. The last thing in the world he needed was to be told that what he was doing was wrong. Whether the criticisms were about the way he was grieving or about what he had done to deserve such a fate, their affect was that of rubbing salt into an open wound.

Job needed sympathy more than he needed advice, even good and correct advice. There would be a time and a place for that later. He needed compassion, the sense that others felt his pain with him, more than he needed wise theological explanations about God's ways. He needed physical comforting, people sharing their strength with him, holding him rather than scolding him.

He needed friends who would permit him to be angry, to cry and to scream, much more than he needed friends who would urge him to be an example of patience and piety to others. He needed people to say, 'Yes, what happened to you is terrible and makes no sense,' not people who would say, 'Cheer up, Job, it's not all that bad.' And that is where his friends let him down. The phrase "Job's comforters" has come into the language to describe people who mean well, but who are more concerned with their own needs and feelings than they are with the grieving person, and end up only making things worse.

Job's friends did at least two things right, though. First of all, they came. I am sure that the prospect of seeing their friend in his misery was painful for them to contemplate, and they must have been tempted to stay away and leave him alone. It's not pleasant to see a friend suffering, and most of us would rather avoid the experience. We either stay away entirely, so that the suffering person experiences isolation and a sense of rejection on top of his tragedy, or we come and try to avoid the reason for our being there. Hospital visits and condolence calls become discussions of the weather, the stock market, or the pennant race, taking on and air of unreality as the most important subject on the mind of everyone present is left conspicuously unmentioned. Job's friends at least mustered the courage to face him and confront his sorrow.

Secondly, they listened. According to the biblical account, they sat with Job several days, not saying anything, while Job wept out of grief and anger. That, I suspect, was the most helpful part of their visit. Nothing they did after that did Job much good. When Job finished his outburst, they should have said, 'Yes that's really awful. We don't know how you put up with it,' instead of feeling compelled to defend God and conventional wisdom. Their silent presence must have been a lot more helpful to their friend than their lengthy theological explanations were. We can all learn a lesson from that".

Even though author Harold Kushner is not a Christian, but a Jewish Rabbi, he confirms to me the overall sense that Job needed help and true compassion—not theological answers. I disagree with some points that Kushner leaves out. He talks about, but does not emphasize the encounter with Satan and the behind-the-scenes look at what was happening in the heavens while pain and suffering were happening on the earth. The New Testament gives further insight into this battle, to which I have already alluded. These insights do not necessarily make it easier to understand pain and suffering, ours and others'—but it brings another dimension to the story of Job and to life in general that actually makes it harder to figure out what is really happening and why. I have heard young people who are somewhat familiar with the book say, "God is playing a cruel joke on the human family. He unleashes Satan on a man to see if he really loves God with all of his soul." This to them, and many of us, seems unfair—but again we have to read and understand the whole book. God is compassionate and does things with true purpose though it doesn't satisfy our human minds.

I have found that everyone suffers in different ways. In my case it is obvious, paralyzed from the waist down, chronic pain, etc. But even before the crash that left me this way, I was in emotional pain because of the things that were not going right for me. I was stuck in a job that was not really what I had envisioned for my life. Even though the job, driving a concrete mixing truck, was not that bad, each day I felt the pressure of wasting time and my life. I had gone to school to be a minister, but through a number of unfortunate circumstances, (read *Walking This Walk*, my first book) I found the concrete job which met our financial needs but left me feeling empty and frustrated. No matter what I did I could not find an opportunity to minister and support my family.

I think it's the same for all of us. You may have the dream job, but be lonely, single or in an unhappy marriage. Your kids may be on drugs even after you taught them that drugs are a dead end road. Your finances may be out of order (like…you're broke); you may have an illness, such as cancer or heart disease. The list goes on and on. God's Word says, "The Lord is near to those who have a broken heart, and saves such who as have a contrite spirit" (Ps 34:18). Everything that is broken externally causes an inward brokenness, a broken heart. When a romantic relationship does not work out, people say they have a broken heart. The physical or exterior loss of the relationship causes the inward emotional or spiritual pain; a broken heart. When we lose things we love, or even just like, we suffer.

Some say we need to be unattached to "things" so we can find our true inner self. Jesus said store your treasures in heaven, "Do not lay up for yourselves treasures on earth, where moth and rust destroy, and where thieves break in and steal; but lay up for yourselves treasures in heaven where neither moth nor rust destroys and where thieves do not break in and steal" (Matt 6:9-20). The idea of "treasure" is grafted into our very being. We all want a profit, to make money. This is not an indictment on materialism—though naked materialism is not right. The idea is to recognize that all that we have we are accountable for. There are more verses in the Bible dealing with money than with heaven and hell. Just like the desire for sexual relationships and marriage are "in" us, so is the idea of financial treasure. What Jesus is emphasizing is storing treasure in heaven and one of the ways we do that is by being good stewards with what God gives us, not necessarily living as monks, (though that is not a bad thing if God calls you to that). The goal of life is not to eliminate desire, which is a Buddhist principle.

Buddhism teaches that we should rid ourselves of all desire, and that if we do, it will eliminate all suffering, because suffering comes from unmet desire. This has some truth to it. If you are able to master yourself to the point that you desire nothing then everything that happens—good or bad—will not matter to you. Many strive to reach this kind of life, even in the Christian world, pointing out that the world is under the power of the evil one so we must not be a part of it at all. This, to many, means that we should not have much feeling in regard to anything, seeing that the world and all that is in it is perishing. So much so that many Christians don't show much real concern for those who are suffering, dying or dead. "Oh well, another one bites the dust." You don't really understand this life fully until you have faced some adversity, and to those who have no feeling about life and suffering I would say you have never had pain, because if you did you would know feeling.

To not have feeling is abnormal. It's not good to be "numb." We don't respond to life properly when we have no feeling or defected feeling. I remember not long after the crash that left me with no movement or feeling below the waist, this truth came to me in an unusual way. We had just gotten back home from an event of some kind, I can't remember where. My wife was driving and I was in the passenger seat. We pulled up to the garage and I got out with everyone's help. I had my leg braces on, so I was able to stand and walk with a walker. The ramp leading to the door was my quest; to get up the ramp with my braces would be a total victory. I was determined to climb this mountain. The problem is when you don't have feeling some things happen that you are not aware of—like your pants falling down! There I was, focused on making my way up the ramp, when my wife and kids said, "Hey! Your pants are down!" Good thing the neighbors weren't out. I don't think anyone saw me, but it was a little embarrassing even though we made a joke out of it. That was Job's friends' problem, they had limited feeling, they had never suffered like him, and so they came to Job with formulas—not true compassionate feeling.

My question again is: Is this the tact the Bible tells us to take in terms of our humanity? To deny that we want things and to eliminate all desire? I don't think so. Contrary to this, it is unmet desire that causes us to reach out to God stronger and with less reservation. To have dreams, plans, finances, health—all these desires are God given. "You have given him his heart's desire, and have not withheld the request of his lips" (Ps 21:2). "Delight yourself also in the Lord, and he shall give you the desires of your heart," (Ps 37:4) meaning that He will plant desires in you so that you will want what He already has planned for your life. God never tells us to lose these desires, but rather to acknowledge our needs and wants, being honest with God and always trusting Him so that if what we want does not come to us, at least not right away, we will not become offended with God. As kids, our parents did everything for us and we found comfort and delight in our needs and many wants being met. When we get older we are asked to pay rent to stay at their house. What changed? Time. Age. The need to take responsibility. Job sat in the lap of luxury until all hell broke loose. He was forced to grow up and see God differently. Job's desires didn't change, he still wanted the good life—what changed was his view and under-standing of God.

We become mature when we become broken to the point where all other desires are subject to one. "One thing I have desired of the Lord, that will I seek; that I may dwell in the house of the Lord all the days of my life, to behold the beauty of the Lord, and to inquire in His temple" (Ps 27:4). As we have seen in the life of David, when things went south, he called on God. He lost everything and recovered it all, he was a man after God's heart, he was broken at various times through-out his life, but he always turned to God, eventual-ly, if not right away. He wrote, *"One thing* I seek...," (emphasis mine) as he suffered loss. Does that mean he had no other desires? That he wanted nothing else? I don't think so. What he was acknowledging was outside of all other desires met or unmet, seek-ing God and experiencing His presence is where real life is. Paul echoes a similar sentiment when he was exasperated by life he came to this point, "One thing I do..." He had it all as a leader of the Pharisees and as man who was respected among his peers. Later, after his conversion, he led a crusade that literally changed the known world in his time and is still changing our world today. But he said,

> "What things were gain to me, these I have counted loss for Christ, yet indeed I also count all things loss for the excellence of the knowledge of Christ Jesus my Lord, for whom I have suffered the loss of all things, and count them as rubbish, that I may gain Christ" (Phil 3:7-8).

He was referring to his credentials as a Pharisee. The title, career and prestige were not leading him to experience more of God. Many have said he was referring to everything as rubbish, but this could not be true. Again this would bring us back to the Buddhist teaching on eliminating all desire. I'm sure he was not referring to the people who were saved under his ministry or any of the good things in life as garbage. But in comparison to any and all good things, Christ and knowing Him is the best life ever. That is what he meant.

It seems that this is where God is taking all of us. To be conformed to His likeness and prepared for the next life.

> "And we know that all things work together for good to those who love God, to those who are the called according to His purpose. For whom He foreknew, He also predestined to be conformed to the image of His Son, that He might be firstborn among many brethren" (Rom 8:28-29).

This verse also tells us, however, that God does not dismiss this life, expecting us to just hold on until the next. He, contrary to the Buddhist philosophy, created us with desires and does not intend that we lose them. He also promises to meet many of them, at the appropriate time. This is one side of the coin. The other side is, even though some, most or all of our natural desires are not met and suffering occurs as a result, He is still there ready to meet our broken hearts with His presence. This is the good news—we can't lose! He will meet many desires, and the many unmet ones are only catalysts that bring us to know God better. The unmet natural desires move us closer to experience more of Him

Think about the dying process. I watched my dad and my father in-law die. I hated it. To see someone you love slowly dissipate right before your eyes is the worst experience ever. As someone is dying though, hopefully, if they have a faith base, they are thinking of what is to come. Some proud and hard hearts may not be thinking about God—but most will be thinking about what's next. Desires will begin to ebb away until finally the desire to live will be given up as well. As we become weaker physically or emotionally it can be a time for God to come closer. Paul says,

> "Therefore most gladly I will rather boast
> in my infirmities, that the power of Christ
> may rest upon me. Therefore I take plea-
> sure in infirmities, in reproaches, in needs,
> in persecutions, in distresses, for Christ's

sake. For when I am weak then I am strong" (2 Cor 12:9b-10).

Many want and cry out for more power, but do not realize that many times it is only through weakness and brokenness that God's power flows. Trials that are designed by God bring about deeper character and identification with His purpose. Rabbi Kushner points out,

> "Man depends on God for all things; God depends on man for one. Without man's love, God does not exist as God, only as creator, and love is the one thing no one— not even God Himself—can command. It is a free gift, or it is nothing. And it is most itself, most free, when it is offered in spite of suffering, of injustice, and of death".

Job loved God for God Himself and no other reason.

I have to disagree with Kushner on his overall perspective of the randomness of what is happening in the world. As with Job we see God allowing Satan to "attack" Job. There is a sense of seeming randomness to what happened to Job, but again, from the scene in heaven we see God's hand in it all. It is almost like he forgot about this event and only focused on Job and his suffering. This puts him in the same camp as author Gregory A. Boyd, who basically says in his book, *Is God to Blame?*, that all the bad that happens does so randomly is not divinely directed. They would both say God is heartbroken by it but not in control of it. It seems that reading the book of Job without reading the first two chapters would bring someone to this conclusion.

Remember what Job said, "Shall we accept good from God and not adversity?" He acknowledged that all—good and bad—comes from God. "You have not spoken what was right of me as my servant Job has" (Job 42:7). God said that. So we have to wonder, unlike Job's friends who said, "It's all your fault Job," how Job understood God is sovereign. To say things happen only randomly, to me, takes God off His throne, the central seat of authority and control. Not control in the sense that He is in a constant motion to stop certain things and let other things go. His control is that He limits things according to His omnipotence. Yes, He has set things in motion, but is fully aware of what is happening and at any point He could change it; most of the time He chooses not to. I remember hearing about Dave Wilkerson's church in Times Square, New York. Weeks before the 9-11 attacks, the church cancelled all the services and went to prayer because they sensed something bad was going to happen. Maybe as a result of their prayers the tragedy was lessened, we really do not know for sure.

I went through a period of thought one time, which basically posited: God doesn't know what is going to happen. The theory goes like this: Paul said that real love hopes all things, so God never created man foreknowing he would fall. Because love hopes, so God hopes—not knowing Adam would sin. True love thinks no evil the Bible says. So according to this, God was taken by surprise when Adam sinned. For God to know Adam would sin would make Him think evil before He created man. I have since rejected this school of thought because it makes God less than all-knowing and all-powerful. Though I acknowledge that God can change His mind and that His omniscience is subject to His will, He is not like a scatter-brained genius whose mind races because of all his knowledge, rather God is at rest with all He knows.

If Christ was crucified from the foundations of the world then it means that God foreknew the fall and pre-designed his plan to save us through His Son. God does not live in space and time; He created it, "For thus says the High and Lofty One Who inhabits eternity" (Is 57:15). He is the eternal God and nothing takes Him by surprise other than what He, by His own volition, chooses not to know. No, He never created the world to suffer, but by making man free moral agents, He made it possible for man to sin and for the pain and suffering of sin's consequences to follow. So it makes more sense to believe in a God who has full control than in a random universe where we are not protected and God is not in control. It's a mystery that God would make all things knowing full well the outcome, but He did. And maybe one reason is that only in this fallen world could love be truly appreciated. Without the fall, and the pain and suffering that went with it, true love could not have been fully realized or tested.

For some this theology of suffering is hard to take, and I know this first hand. My kids are very inquisitive, asking why God would allow me to be paralyzed. My first answer is that God is God and I am not. This is not a cop out, as I have discussed what I believe in terms of His control over all things. I find that this thought leaves them unsatisfied though; it doesn't line up in their heads—they still have kid minds. Paul said, "When I was a child I spoke as a child, I understood as a child, I thought as a child, but when I became a man I put away childish things" (1 Cor 13:11). When a person stops thinking like a child varies in different cultures; sometimes I wonder when kids in America will ever grow up. Unfortunately, there are fifty year olds who still think like children. Part of growing up means that you have thought through issues and have a maturity that enables you to accept things that you do not understand—trusting that God has His hand on all things. Or if you accept the random view, you can trust that God is with you in all things. You can accept confusion or not knowing by faith, realizing that whatever you accept in terms of God and suffering will never be 100% absolute. It must be accepted by faith. I accept that the Bible is inspired by God and that it is the final word, period. Reason and logic, through open-minded study, point to this conclusion, and the Holy Spirit also gives us understanding, and with our more mature minds helps us accept it by faith.

It is amazing to me that people will trust their own understanding and yet never question where that understanding comes from. They will look at the world and science and accept certain conclusions that they make but never ask what is behind the scenes. The agnostic says, "I don't believe we can know that God exists with absolute certainty." They are totally convinced about this. Okay, so you are absolutely convinced that you do not know. Do you see the nonsensical logic of this view? You are sure of something that you do not know. Well, I am sure of what I do know and have come to believe is true through research of history and the Bible, and reason. Although discoveries in science and archaeology continue to point toward the truth of the Bible and the existence of God—complete belief is still a faith step. Where the agnostic has faith that he does not know, I have faith in what I do know.

There are many things in the Bible that we do not understand. I talked to my sister the other day and she told me of a good friend of hers who was once a Christian but now questions the faith. She raised questions about Noah and all the people who did not get in the ark. She talked about many Old Testament stories where it appeared God was unjust and many died innocently. Why would David kill so many at God's command and then be disqualified from building the temple because he was a "man of war?" Just because there seems to be things that may contradict the character of God, it doesn't mean that they really do. A closer look may reveal things about God's ways that are quite amazing. David writes, "The Lord executes righteousness and justice for all who are oppressed. He made known His ways to Moses, His acts to the children of Israel" (Ps 103:6-7). It is possible to see the creation and believe in God. Romans chapters one and two indicate this, but to know His ways is not that easy. True, it is belief that gets us in the door so to speak, but it is a lifetime of walking with God and studying the Word that will enable us to know His ways. So instead of tossing out Christianity as a whole because of certain things that don't make sense to you, it would be wiser to admit to not understanding, ask God for revelation and seek for answers.

Skeptics do bring up issues. I heard many during my days of preaching on college campuses. Many times it is not about God's word per se (most have never read it) but about Christianity through the centuries. Why did the Christians kill people they thought were witches, or create a religious system that oppressed poor people? Or why did the white European Christians come to America and kill the Native Americans? All of these deserve an answer. History, especially liberal history (the kind they teach in public schools and universities) does not paint Christianity in a very good light. When I hear these arguments I want to compare what happened then to what Jesus of Nazareth taught. Actually, He taught opposite of this, "...love your enemies, bless those who curse you, do good to those who hate you, and pray for those who spitefully use you and persecute you" (Matt 5:44).

It sounds simplistic, but it brings the attention back to where it should be, Jesus. Who was He? What did He teach, and what should I do about it? This is the struggle of the human heart. Because it comes back to the heart, the inner central core of who you are. The Pharisees had sharp minds, they knew the Bible. Jesus said of them, "You search the scriptures for in them you think you have eternal life; and these are they which testify of Me, but you are unwilling to come to Me that you may have life" (John 5:39-40). They missed Him, but they knew what was written. Here is the fine line in my estimation.

This interpretation of the Word debate has been going on for centuries. Recently in America the Azusa Street Revival, which began in 1906 and continued until roughly 1915, swung the pendulum from the study of and application of the Word, to finding the "move of the Spirit" using the Word and "inner light." (Azusa Street in Los Angeles was a where many believe the charismatic/Pentecostal movement, which stresses speaking in tongues, healing and personal prophecy, began.) The problem was that the Word and the Spirit came into conflict with each other rather than complementing each other. This has created a rift, or a division in the sense that many see healing, prosperity and other issues as black and white, and leave no room for disagreement. Faith churches see it one way, mainline or Bible-based churches see another way. As a member of "Faith" churches most of my Christian life, and as a graduate from "Mainline" Christian colleges, I have felt this discord first hand. I have struggled through it, and have been able to make some determinations on what I believe.

I want to finish this section with an admonition and some encouragement. Why certain things happen while you walk with God is a mystery. Even if you did have answers to your issues and problems they would not leave you with relief. This is well noted by Kushner in *When Bad Things Happen to Good People*,

> "Is there an answer to the question of why bad things happen to good people? That depends on what we mean by 'answer.' If we mean, is there an explanation which will make sense of it all?—'why is there cancer in the world, or why did my child die?'—then there is probably no satisfying answer. We can offer learned explanations, but in the end, when we have covered all the squares on the game board and are feeling very proud of our cleverness, the pain and the anguish and the sense of unfairness will still be there".

Kushner believes that God is not perfect and that we should accept this as we attempt to move on in life. We should "forgive" God for not being perfect. As for me, I do not worship a flawed God, an imperfect being who is sometimes caught by surprise by the world that He created. No, the God I seek to know is beyond my understanding and His ways are beyond my reasoning. "Oh the depth of the riches both of the wisdom and knowledge of God! How unsearchable are His judgments and His ways past finding out" (Rom 11:33). Paul, who knew the Old Testament very well, came to this glorious conclusion, *"His ways are past finding out."* Remember, the nation of Israel knew the deeds of God, the things He did, but Moses knew the ways of God. Deeds and ways are two different things. A child may see his dad do various things, like build a table or a chair or a house. He may be very impressed with how his dad can do these things. Yet when his dad says or does things he does not understand he may doubt him, even though what his dad is doing is in his best interest. It is the same in our relationship with God. We are amazed at the world He made but dumbfounded by the things that don't seem to add up.

God is not pushing for a Holy war, telling us to worship cows, or inviting us to a life where we seek to free ourselves from all desire thus all suffering. None of these explanations will do. Why bad things happen is the same reason why Adam and Eve ate from the tree. Choice. Free will. God can, but chooses not to, violate this sacred right that He has given the human family. This is what gives life its true mystery. Life is to be lived with great joy and love for God and to seek to know the mystery of His ways.

When all is said and done we are left with our life, God and the world we live in. Our circumstances can change for better or worse. Our life and our relationship with God is what will keep us grounded when hard times come. Our understanding of God and His ways will increase as we read and follow what we believe is God's will for us. You will ask why, and you may get some answers, and hopefully like Paul, you will be able to move forward in the fact that God's grace is sufficient for you. Your pain will hopefully recede as you accept—by faith—God's will and direction for your life. Your pain may never fully go away but God's comfort will not leave you, although you may not feel it all the time. "Blessed be the God and Father of our Lord Jesus Christ, the Father of mercies and God of all comfort, who comforts us in all our tribulation" (2 Cor 1:3-4a). This is what I've found is the most important thing to realize, and hardest to keep applying on a consistent basis. But God promises a new life for those who accept Him and this life is His gift that He will not rescind. "...I will never leave you nor forsake you" (Heb 13:3b).

Chapter 6

Faith in the Wrong Understanding

Let's go back to the story of Job and his comforters. Eliphaz starts off with words of encouragement, reminding Job that he was a blessing to many, "Surely you have strengthened weak hands, your words have upheld him who was stumbling. And you have strengthened feeble knees" (Job 4:3-4). Job, you're a great guy, you're valuable, you matter. That's good. He should have stopped there, but he goes on. "Remember now, who ever perished being innocent? Or were the upright ever cut off? Even as I have seen, those who plow in iniquity and sow trouble reap the same" (Job 4:7-8). Where did this come from? You just sat with this man for seven days and nights and this is what you've have come up with? Think about it, this thought process must have been brewing in his mind for most of the time he sat with Job. Eliphaz wanted to lay it down to Job this way, "You must have done something to deserve this; your wrong actions are why this is happening."

Scholars disagree on exactly when this book was written, but Eliphaz was getting his thoughts from somewhere. He may have read Deuteronomy chapter twenty-eight about the blessings and cursings and concluded that Job had disobeyed God. Remember that Job was pronounced righteous by God in the beginning so Eliphaz was only assuming this about Job. Or maybe this was oral tradition that was passed down. That's how history was preserved back then; there were no printing presses. Things took a great deal of time to write down. Eventually it did get written down, but in the meantime the story was passed orally from one to another. Many see God in the Old Testament as a God of wrath, and His mercy, though it is present, is not front and center for sure. This could be where Eliphaz is getting his ideas from, we don't know for sure. I want to jump over to the New Testament for a minute. Sometimes things do come to us for our disobedience.

Some use Communion, the Lord's Supper, as a sort of piety weather vane, misusing the following passage from Paul's letter to the Corinthians with the wrong intent. "For he who eats and drinks in an unworthy manner eats and drinks judgment to himself, not discerning the Lord's body. For this reason many are weak and sick among you, and many sleep" (1 Cor 11:29-30). Many have used this as a club to demolish hurting people. "Well, you must not be taking the Lord's Supper properly; you must have sin in your life, that's the reason for your troubles." This could be true—but is it always? I don't think so. Job's life shows us another side of suffering. Pain and suffering are not one dimensional. There are more far-reaching purposes for suffering. Paul is offering encouragement when he says, "For if we would judge ourselves, we would not be judged" (1 Cor 11:31). Thank God the purpose of the Lord's Supper is to repent of sin and embrace the cross for forgiveness. These people that Paul was referring to were flippant and not respectful of God or their fellow man. This is not the case with Job, by Eliphaz's own admission Job was helpful to many, and he was outwardly upright.

Eliphaz goes on with his perspective,

> "For wrath kills a foolish man, and envy slays a simple one. I have seen the foolish taking root, but suddenly I cursed his dwelling place. His sons are far from safety, they are crushed in the gate, and there is no deliverer...but as for me I would seek God...He sets on high those who are lowly and those who mourn are lifted to safety... behold happy is the man whom God corrects; therefore do not despise the chastening of the Almighty. For he bruises, but he binds up; He wounds, but his hands make whole. He shall deliver you in six troubles; yes in seven no evil shall touch you" (Job 5:2-4, 11, 17-19).

In other words, "Job, don't you know God and His ways? Just believe and He will turn it all around." It sounds like faith movement teaching—and it is. Too bad the context is never mentioned when many of these false teachings are espoused.

What Eliphaz is saying is not totally wrong, in fact there is truth to much of what he said, but the application was wrong. Like Satan in the wilderness with Jesus, quoting actual scripture to Jesus, but out of context. God never intends to make a suffering person feel worse—never. It is true that if you do things God's way you may prosper and be in health, but you may also go through difficult times like the early Christians. "Still others had trials of mocking and scourging, yes and of chains and imprisonment. They were stoned, they were sawn in two; they were slain with the sword" (Heb 11:36-37). These people went through brutal times but maintained their faith, in fact the writer of Hebrews goes on to say of them, "...of whom the world was not worthy" (Heb 11:38a). When a viewpoint is just one way, one extreme, it is usually wrong. Eliphaz had one idea, Job was suffering because of his sin, he saw no other option. To him it was black and white; no gray, no colors, no hews, no multifaceted wisdom of God. Paul states that God's wisdom is many sided,

> "To me, who am less than least of all the saints, this grace was given, that I should preach among the Gentiles the unsearchable riches of Christ and to make all see what is fellowship of the mystery which from ages has been hidden in God who created all things through Jesus Christ; to the intent that now the manifold wis-

dom of God might be made known by the
church to the principalities and powers in
the heavenly places" (Eph 3:8-10).

Think about it. Eliphaz did not have the understanding of what was going on in heaven while Job
was suffering on earth; there was no book of Job for
reference. If Eliphaz had known what was taking
place behind the scenes, more than likely he would
have had a whole different train of thought.
Job makes a big mistake, one we all make when we
feel attacked, he became defensive. Job begins to defend his righteousness and rants about what is happening to him.

> "Oh, that my grief were fully weighed, and
> my calamity laid with it on the scales! For
> then it would be heavier than the sand of
> the sea—therefore my words have been
> rash. For the arrows of the Almighty are
> within me; my spirit drinks in their poison;
> the terrors of God are against me" (Job 6:2-
> 4).

In other words, God is against me, what are you
talking about? "To him who is afflicted kindness
should be shown by his friend, even if he forsakes the
fear of the Almighty. My brothers have dealt deceit-
fully like a brook, like the streams of the brooks that
pass away" (Job 6:14-15). Even if a man is not a believer, you should never say to him, "God is judging
you for your sins." Job is a believer and still he feels

attacked and feels the need to defend himself. "How forceful are your right words! But what does your arguing prove? Yield now, let there be no injustice! Yes, concede, my righteousness still stands! Is there injustice on my tongue?" (Job 6:25, 29-30).

Job is hurting. Just to remind ourselves of his pain listen to what he says.

> "Therefore I will not restrain my mouth;
> I will speak in the anguish of my spirit; I
> will complain in the bitterness of my soul.
> Am I a sea, or a sea serpent, that You set a
> guard over me? When I say, my bed will
> comfort me, my couch will ease my com-
> plaint, then You scare me with dreams and
> terrify me with visions, so that my soul
> chooses strangling and death rather than
> my body. I loath my life; I would not live
> forever. Let me alone, for my days are but
> a breath" (Job 6:11-16).

Job has shifted his focus to God, he goes back and forth from defending his righteousness to crying out to God about His harsh treatment of him.

> "What is man that You should exalt him,
> that You should set Your heart on him,
> that You should visit him every morning,
> and test him every moment? How long?
> Will You not look away from me, and let
> me alone till I swallow my saliva? Have I
> sinned? What have I done to You O watch-

er of men? Why have You set me as Your
target" (Job 6:17-20).

This is how many people feel when they are going through trials; Job just happens to be willing to
admit it. He feels singled out by God and wonders
what he has done to deserve such harsh treatment. I
have heard some say that they never questioned God
or were upset when bad times came. I guess that's
a good thing if you can do that, but most can't. The
mind does not work that way, it questions, it doubts,
it wonders—and yes—it wanders in many different
directions. God is patient with the wonderings and
wanderings as we will continue to see.

Job's next buddy is going to begin his speech.

> "Then Bildad the Shuite answered and
> said: "How long will you speak these
> things, and the words of your mouth be like
> a strong wind? Does God subvert judg-
> ment? Or does the Almighty pervert jus-
> tice? ...if you were pure and upright, surely
> now He would awake for you, and prosper
> your rightful dwelling place. Though your
> beginning was small, yet your latter end
> would increase abundantly" (Job 8:1-3, 6-
> 7).

Again this sounds like much of the teaching that
we hear today. If you put God first, God will bless

you. If you're not blessed then it's because you have not put Him first. Plain and simple, that's it. Even if it is not said forthrightly, the undercurrent still flows in this direction. Beware of a preacher who has never suffered on some level. Not to say that just because they haven't makes them less, because that would be using the same logic in the opposite direction. But it is true that suffering makes people sensitive to others' plight. I used to feel bad for people in wheelchairs but now that I am in one, I can relate on a whole new level. It is hard to say if Bildad had ever suffered loss on any level because the Bible doesn't say. But I doubt that he had, he is arrogant and self righteous and totally out of touch with the depths of Job's pain. "So are the paths of all who forget God; and the hope of the hypocrite shall perish, whose confidence shall be cut off, and whose trust is a spider's web" (Job 8:13). He continues to insinuate that Job has "forgotten God."

After talking about God and His greatness, justice and power, Job goes back to ranting about how God has done this to him. "For He crushes me with tempest, and multiplies my wounds without cause" (Job 8:17). He then goes back to defending his righteousness. "I am blameless, yet I do not know myself; I despise my life. It is all one thing; therefore I say He destroys the blameless and the wicked" (Job 8:21-22). Job is still trying to figure it all out. He says he is blameless but he doesn't really know himself, so maybe he isn't. Then he says God destroys the blameless and the wicked anyway, so what is the point? "I despise my life." Job said, "I am afraid of all my sufferings; I know that

You will not hold me innocent. If I am condemned, why then do I labor in vain?" (Job 8:28-29). It seems that he is going back and forth, though he defends his righteousness to his friends at times he seems unsure about it. If God would just take this suffering away from him, it would be easier to move forward. "Let Him take His rod away from me, and do not let dread of Him terrify me. Then I would speak and not fear Him, but it is not so with me" (Job 9:34-35).

We all stumble in many ways, (James 3:2) and, though we are exhorted to be single minded, many times we are not. I heard one person say you cannot think about two things at once. I think this is false, you can think about many things simultaneously. Job is thinking about defending his righteousness, moaning against God for doing this to him, and wondering about it, all at the same time. We should all attempt to be as single minded as possible, and it is true that we will go in the direction of our most dominant thoughts. The thoughts that are most on our minds will be the ones we follow. This is really what Job is struggling with, to maintain the proper thoughts amidst all his pain.

The third friend, Zophar the Naamthite, begins his discourse.

> "Should not the multitude of words be answered? And should a man full of talk be vindicated? Should your empty talk make men hold their peace? And when you mock, should no one rebuke you? For

you have said, my doctrine is pure and I
am clean in your eyes. But oh, that God
would speak, and open his lips against
you, that He would show you the secrets
of wisdom! For they would double your
prudence. Know therefore that God exacts
from you less than your iniquity deserves"
(Job 11:2-6).

It seems that, as the third person to speak, the
"truth" has been building up within him. He comes
out with guns blazing and makes his case. He then
gives Job the prescription for deliverance.

"If you would prepare your heart, and
stretch out your hands toward Him; if iniquity were in your hand, and you would put
it far away, and would not let wickedness
dwell in your tents; then surely you could
lift up your face without spot; yes, you
could be steadfast, and not fear; because
you would forget your misery, and remember it as waters that have passed away, and
your life would be brighter than noonday.
Though you were dark, you would be like
the morning" (Job 11:13-17).

To sum it up, "Job you're sinning, stop and you will
be healed." I like Job's response to this. "No doubt
you are the people, and wisdom will die with you!"
(Job 12:2). In other words, "You guys are definitely
God's men, you have the wisdom, and I will listen to

you." The Pharisees of the New Testament times were also very upright—externally anyway. Jesus called them, "whitewashed tombs, blind guides, hypocrites" (Matt 23). If you wanted to categorize Job's friends, "Pharisees" is quite an apt label. When Christ came, the Pharisees missed Him because of their theology. Job's friends were missing the point, also blinded by their theology.

John chapter nine is the story about the man born blind. The disciples came to Jesus with questions, "Who sinned, this man or his parents?" (John 9:2). The idea of someone's sin was assumed, someone is responsible for this and it can't be God, so it has to be someone who has done wrong. The man was healed by Jesus and brought to the Pharisees. The Pharisees were so interested in the cause of the man's blindness that they forgot about the man. Jesus said, concerning the sin issue, no one has sinned, this blindness was for God's glory.

> "Neither this man nor his parents sinned, but that the works of God should be revealed in him. I must work the works of Him who sent me while it is day, the night is coming when no man can work. As long as I am in the world, I am the light of the world" (John 9:3-5).

He healed the blind man, and instead of being glad that the man could see, they argued about healing on the Sabbath.

"Therefore some of the Pharisees said, this Man is not from God, because He does not keep the Sabbath. Others said, 'How can a man who is a sinner do such signs?' And there was a division among them" (John 9:16).

They went back and forth for a while and the Pharisee's asked the man again about his healing. The man said, "'Why, this is a marvelous thing, that you do not know where He is from; yet He has opened my eyes'" (John 9:30).

The Pharisee's could not put Jesus into their mental framework. They were looking for a Messiah who was strong and mighty and that upheld what they believed about Moses and the Sabbath. The One they were looking for was to destroy their enemies and set up His kingdom on earth. They could not accept Jesus was the Messiah. The man born blind was making the argument that Jesus could not do these things if He were not sent from God. They rejected his argument because of who he was, "They answered and said to him, 'You were completely born in sin, and you are teaching us?' And they cast him out" (John 9:34). They rejected the truth because of the package that it came in. They were unwilling to see it in a different way. That's how Job's friends were as well. They could not see Job's suffering any way other than as a result of sin. Many in our age of superstars and perfect athletes and actors have fallen prey to this. If Joe Average Christian says it, it has little effect; we need the

Christian superstars to say it. Even though Job came out on top, while he was under the pain of his trial, no one wanted to look at him as a role model or someone to follow. After all, he is a defeated man, not worthy of God, and is making God look bad. That is why we cannot judge things before they come full circle.

Job continued to Zophar,

> "But I have understanding as well as you; I am not inferior to you. Indeed, who does not know such things as these? I am one mocked by his friends, who called on God, and He answered him, the just and blameless who is ridiculed" (Job 12:3-4).

He goes on,

> "What you know, I also know, I am not inferior to you, but I would speak to the Almighty, and desire to reason with God, but you are forgers of lies, you are all worthless physicians. Oh, that you would be silent, and it would be your wisdom!" (Job 13:2-4).

Job is stooping further down to their level. You sense he is getting more frustrated with the constant barrage of stupid, off-hand rhetoric. He even, in this case, stoops to name calling, "you are all worthless physicians." Comparing and contrasting is always a trap, but this is where he was going, "I am not inferior to you."

I was talking to a man whose sister is taking driving lessons to be a truck driver. He is a self-taught truck driver and was asking her if they had taught her this or that aspect of driving. She was not learning it the way he thought she should. He was saying that this was like religion, everyone is taught something different. He was a little confused about the God issue and was trying to figure it all out. I asked him, "Are there textbooks that teach the basics of driving?" He admitted that there were. "So, go by the book," I said to him. If you're confused about all the religions, pick up the Book and read it for yourself. If a drunk in the street is preaching the death, burial and resurrection of Jesus according to the scriptures, his lifestyle does not change the truth. The truth is the truth no matter what. Yes, if you're going to preach the Gospel you should live in a manner worthy of the Gospel, but your life, your devotion, your prayers, your good works will not, and does not alter what happened two thousand years ago.

So Job's friends may have been living right, but they were not speaking right. They were healthy and wealthy, (if you can leave your life for weeks at a time to be with a friend, you have to have some money) and some of what they taught was truth, but it was not applied correctly. Job's friends were in fact trying to defend God, so much that they forgot about Job. This is what was so frustrating to Job, and he reproached them,

> "Will you speak wickedly for God, and talk deceitfully for Him? Will you show partiality for Him? Will you contend for God? Will it be well when He searches you out? Or can you mock Him like one mocks a man? He will surely rebuke you if you secretly show partiality. Will not His excellence make you afraid, and the dread of Him falls upon you? Your platitudes are proverbs of ashes, your defenses are defenses of clay" (Job 13:7-12).

Job is continuing down their low road, and is defending himself and confronting them about what they believe about God. In essence he was saying, "What the heck is wrong with you guys? I am in all this pain, and you are worried about how God looks? Why can't you offer me something that will help my situation?"

Chapter 7

A More Reasoned Faith Response

This back and forth goes on until "the words of Job are ended" (Job 31:40). "So these men ceased answering Job, because he was righteous in his own eyes" (Job 32:1). The "friends" ended their talk because they determined that it was a hopeless cause. They reasoned that they had done all they could do to get through to him, so—oh well. It reminds me of people who want to convert others to Jesus—this is a good thing, and do not misunderstand me in this. I wanted so badly to make people believe, that for years I would crusade with an "in your face" attitude. I went street and campus preaching, earnestly contending for the faith, putting people on the spot, confronting their unbelief and disregard for truth. In these settings you can not afford to let your guard down because the skeptics will run over you quickly, so these tactics had a specific purpose. I really only wanted to reach them on their own turf. People would say that I was being too hard, but I thought they were just being soft on sin and not willing to make a stand. Looking back, I am not ashamed of my approach or what went on in these debates. They were lively discussions and yes, at times we may have gotten a little "over zealous". But all told it was a good learning experience.

I know for a fact though, that we missed the mark, at times wanting only to win arguments and not hearts. You can win a debate without winning the person to Jesus. For that setting, that was the proper method, but for the day to day relationships with people it is important to build a connection with them in order to win them to Jesus. "I become all things to all men so that I may win them" (1 Cor 9:19-23). Back then, however, when I would hear people talk like this, I would think they were just being wimpy. I have since seen that to be sensitive to God and to each individual person is just as important as the gospel you preach, and this could ultimately win a person over more than sound argumentation. "Let nothing be done through selfish ambition or conceit, but in lowliness of mind let each esteem others better than himself. Let each of you look out not only for his own interests but also the interests of others" (Phil 2:3-4). (But I do still love to debate skeptics!)

Job's friends were interested in defending God (winning the argument) and putting Job in his proper place—as if God needs humans to defend Him. Like a flea defending an elephant. We certainly don't want God to look bad, but does He really need us, puny man, to defend Him? I want to bring sound argumentation to the issues of life and yes, we are God's ambassadors, called to teach and preach God's word. God and the people we speak with are responsible for the rest. We are presenters and tellers but it is impossible for us to decide for man what he will choose. God must sweep through the human soul and bring His renewal and direction and man must respond. This is the experience that is being set up for Job, but a few things still need to happen.

A man named Elihu begins his exhortation.

> "Then the wrath of Elihu, the son of Barachel the Buzite of the family of Ram, was aroused against Job; his wrath was aroused because he [Job] justified himself rather than God. And against his three friends his wrath was aroused, because they had found no answer, and yet had condemned Job" (Job 32:2-3).

Here is how he begins his speech,

> "I am young in years and you are very old. Therefore I was afraid and dared not declare my opinion to you. I said, age should speak, and multitude of years should teach wisdom. But there is a spirit in man, and the breath of the Almighty gives him understanding. Great men are not always wise, nor do the aged always understand justice" (Job 32:6-9).

If there is any question about the sum of what is happening these verses should put it all right. Job is defending himself rather than God against the friends' accusations. Eliphaz, Bildad and Zophar cannot find a satisfactory way to refute Job, which Elihu also finds tantamount to condemning God. The youngest of the group, Elihu is amazed, and concludes that just because a person is older does not mean he is wiser. There really is no fool like an old fool.

Elihu does not seem to be coming from the same perspective as the others. He says, "Now he has not directed his words to me; so I will not answer him with your words" (Job 32:14). Elihu is saying, "Job is not talking directly to me so I will not answer him like you guys." (Paraphrased) By his own words he seems to be humble and God fearing,

> "I will speak, that I may find relief; I must open my lips and answer, let me not, I pray show partiality to anyone, nor let me flatter any man...please, Job, hear my speech and listen to all my words...my words come from my upright heart; my lips utter pure knowledge. The Spirit of God has made me, and the breath of the Almighty gives me life...truly I am your spokesman before God; I also have been formed out of clay. Surely no fear of me will terrify you, nor will my hand be heavy on you" (Job 32:21-33:7).

He is assuring Job that he is just a man and the Spirit of God gives him life. He is, by his own account, upright in heart. He is on Job's side, let there be no doubt about this. Author Ruth Tucker writes about this man in her book *God Talk*.

> "He [Elihu] is not only angry with Job, but he is also angry with the three friends for their inability to refute Job. Some commentators have suggested that this last speaker has little new to offer, I disagree. Elihu speaks more pointedly than do the others to the issue of the silence of God. In chapter 34, he says of God: 'But if He remains silent, who can condemn Him? If He hides his face, who can see Him?' (v29) In some ways, that says it all. What if God were to give a response to the problem of pain? The problem of evil? Would the answers solve the problem? Wouldn't answers be a setup for condemnation? But if He remains silent, who can condemn Him?". (I'll discuss this subject more later.)

Elihu states, "I also will declare my opinion" (Job 32:10). So even though he has the spirit of God, and the breath of the Almighty is in him, there is still a sense that he is a man and that what he is about to offer is only his opinion. This is where we need the Spirit of God in order to gain the right understanding. This is fundamental—yet so often overlooked—especially in the Charismatic/Pentecostal sections of Christendom. They often look at a verse and if it "pops out" at them they will take it and run with it, many times to their and others' detriment. The Apostle Paul said to study...so we must see it in context then ask God to give us the correct application. Not all the word of God is to be applied directly, as the book of Job shows us. (This is a significant point that I want us to really get, so it bears repeating.)

Elihu assures Job that he has heard him,

> "Surely you have spoken in my hearing, and I have heard the sound of your words, saying, 'I am pure, without transgression, I am innocent, and there is no iniquity in me. Yet He finds occasions against me, He counts me as His enemy; He puts my feet in the stocks, He watches all my paths'" (Job 33:8-11).

Elihu is confident that he knows what Job is talking about; he hears him and feels his pain. He is not buying Job's argument, though. He is not going to commit to Job's idea of righteousness. The Bible says, "There is none righteous, no not one" (Rom 3:10).

> "Truly there is not one person on the earth whose heart is pure; we are all infected by sin. "Look, in this you are not righteous. I will answer you, for God is greater than man. Why do you contend with Him? For He does not give an accounting of any of His words. For God may speak in one way,

or in another. Yet man does not perceive it,
in a dream, in a vision of the night, when
deep sleep falls upon men, while slumber-
ing on their beds, then He opens the ears
of men, and seals their instruction. In order to turn man from his deed, and conceal
pride from man, He keeps back his soul
from the Pit, and his life from perishing by
the sword" (Job 33:12-18).

His theology appears to be the same as the friends;
however, his motive seems to be different. He really
wants to absolve Job, "If you have anything to say,
answer me; speak, for I desire to justify you" (Job
33:32).

Elihu speaks to everyone present, "Therefore listen to me you men of understanding" (Job 34:10). He
begins to defend God also,

"Far be it from God to do wickedness, and
for the Almighty to commit iniquity. For
He repays man according to his work, and
makes man to find a reward according to
his way. Surely God will never do wick-
edly, nor will the Almighty pervert justice"
(Job 34:10-12).

The theme of God punishing the wicked and re-
warding the just is one of the main thrusts of his argument. God is just and will do as He pleases; He needs
no justification for what He does. He speaks against
Job to the friends,

> "Men of understanding say to me, wise men who listen to me, Job speaks without knowledge, his words are without wisdom. Oh that Job were tried to the utmost, because his answers are like those of wicked men! For he adds rebellion to his sin, he claps his hands among us, and multiplies his words against God" (Job 34:34-37).

Job had definitely defended his own righteousness to be sure, which elicits this negative response from Elihu. I must admit that I wonder about the appropriateness of Elihu's charge, but I have to think that he was moving in the right direction, because in the end when God rebuked the friends, He says nothing about Elihu. That makes me think that although Elihu sounds like the others, he is not the same. The silence of God issue that was mentioned is also quite a solid insight that deserves thought. God is not speaking at the moment, and in His silence the voices of men are being heard loud and clear.

He continues,

> "Do you think this is right? Do you say, 'My righteousness is more than God's?' For you say, 'What advantage will it be to You? What profit shall I have, more than if I had sinned?' I will answer you, and your companions with you...if you sin, what do you accomplish against Him? Or if your transgressions are multiplied, what do you

accomplish against Him? If you are righteous, what do you give Him? Or, what does He receive from your hand?" (Job 35:6-7).

He goes on,
"...surely God will not listen to empty talk, nor will the Almighty regard it. Although you say you do not see Him, yet justice is before Him and you must wait for Him. And now, because He has not punished in His anger, nor taken much notice of folly, therefore Job opens his mouth in vain, he multiplies words without knowledge" (Job 35:13-16).

Elihu seems to be trying to show Job the folly of affirming his own righteousness and not trusting God's. "Bear with me a little, and I will show you, that there are still words to speak on God's behalf...behold God is mighty, but despises no one" (Job 36:2, 5). He magnifies the power of God,

"Behold God is great, and we do not know Him, nor can the number of His years be discovered...God thunders marvelously with His voice, He does great things which we cannot comprehend...listen to this, O Job, stand still and consider wondrous works of God" (Job 36:26, 37:5, 14).

He continues to talk about God's creation and ends his discourse with these words, "As for the Almighty, we cannot find Him; He is excellent in power. In judgment and abundant justice, He does not oppress, therefore men fear Him, He shows no partiality to any who are wise of heart" (Job 37:23-24). It appears that Elihu is speaking along the same lines as the others, however, the spirit behind what he is saying is directed to Job, while it seems Eliphaz, Bildad and Zophar expounded just so that God would hear their sermons. As we will see in the next chapter, God tells them about the same thing.

Chapter 8

When God Speaks Job (and Everyone Else) Listens

"Then the Lord answered Job out of the whirlwind, and said" (Job 38:1). Okay, now the Lord is going to talk, we should perk up and listen intently. Notice all of what was said up to this point, though it is "God breathed" scripture, it is not God talking; it is Job and his friends. Now we have God Himself speaking, so we'd better get it right here. God starts this discourse like this,

> "Who is this who darkens counsel by words without knowledge? Now prepare yourself like a man; I will question you and you shall answer Me. Where were you when I laid the foundation of the earth? Tell Me, if you have understanding. Who determined its measurements? Surely you know! Or who stretched the line upon it? To what were its foundations fashioned? Or who laid its cornerstone. When the morning stars sang together, and all the sons of God shouted for joy" (Job 38:2-7).

God is revealing the magnitude of His power in these verses, His ability to create all things from nothing…which He did before He even thought of creating Job.

"Where were you, Job," God asks, "before I made all this? Have you commanded the morning since your days began, and caused the dawn to know its place? That it might take hold of the ends of the earth, and the wicked be shaken out of it? It takes on form like clay under a seal, and stands out like a garment. From the wicked their light is withheld, and the upraised arm is broken. Have you entered the springs of the sea? Or have you walked in search of the depths? Have the gates of death been revealed to you? Or have you seen the doors of the shadow of death? Have you commanded the breadth of the earth? Tell Me, if you know all this" (Job 38:12-18).

The Lord continues His argument about His greatness and Job's smallness. Okay, God we know you're awesome, Job may be thinking, but how does that help me, it is only making me feel small. It's like when you were little and your dad would scold you for something, making reference to his hard work and financial commitment to the family. If God is saying these things you must believe that He has a very good reason.

He continues in chapter thirty-nine.

"Do you know the time when the wild mountain goats beat young? Or can you mark where the deer gives birth? Can you number the months that they fulfill? Or do you know the time when they bear young? They bow down, they bring forth their young, they deliver their offspring, their young ones are healthy, they grow strong with grain they depart and do not return to them...have you given the horse strength? Have you clothed his neck with thunder? Can you frighten him like a locust? His majestic snorting strikes terror. He paws in the valley, and rejoices in his strength; He gallops into the clash of arms. He mocks at fear and is not frightened. Nor does he turn back from the sword...does the hawk fly by your wisdom, and spread its wings toward the south? Does the eagle mount up at your command, and make its nest on high?" (Job 39:1-4, 19-22, 26, 27).

Again God is appealing to His ability to create and keep track of tremendous animals and majestic birds. Job is probably scratching his head at this point. But after he thinks about it I think some things are finally starting to settle in on him. So after all of this great adversity that has come to him, from the loss of family, health, self respect and a feeling of wonderment at what God was doing, something is about to click.

"Moreover the Lord answered Job, and said, 'Shall the one who contends with the Almighty correct Him? [Ouch] He who rebukes God let him answer it'" (Job 40:1, 2). It seems that God is taking all of Job's complaints as an insult to who He is. We don't usually think of our doubts and questions as an affront to God—and thank God (literally), He is very patient with us. But it seems in this case that he is a little offended at Job for his remarks. When God speaks, Job listens. "Then Job answered the Lord and said, 'Behold I am vile; what shall I answer You? I lay my hand over my mouth. Once I have spoken, but I will not answer, yes twice, but I will proceed no further'" (Job 40:3-5). Although Job feels bad about everything, he feels bad primarily about his reaction to God about his trial.

"Then the Lord answered Job out of the whirlwind, and said, "Now prepare yourself like a man; I will question you and you shall answer Me. Would you indeed annul my judgment? Would you condemn Me that you may be justified? Have you an arm like God? Or can you thunder with a voice like His? Then adorn yourself with majesty and splendor, and array yourself with glory and beauty. Disperse the rage of your wrath, look on everyone who is proud, and humble him. Look on everyone who is proud and bring him low; tread down the wicked in their place. Hide them in the dust together; bind their faces in hidden darkness. Then I will also confess to you that your own right hand can save you'" (Job 40:6-14).

God is saying, "Who are you Job, really?" James says our life is a vapor here on earth. Heaven is a different story, but here on earth, we are alive only for a brief time. You are not like Me Job, "For My thoughts are not your thoughts, nor are your ways My ways, says the Lord. For as the heavens are higher than the earth, so are My ways higher than your ways and My thoughts than your thoughts" (Is 55:8-9). In other words, "My thoughts are not your thoughts Job; you don't think like Me and you can't do what I can." God is telling of His ability to humble proud people and put the "wicked in their place." Some people think they are called to put people in their place, but in reality, over the long haul, only God can do that.

"Look now at the Behemoth, which I made along with you; he eats grass like an ox. See now, his strength is in his hips, and his power is in his stomach muscles. He moves his tail like a cedar; the sinews of his thighs are tightly knit...can you draw out Leviathan with a hook, or snare his tongue with a line which you lower...can you fill his skin with harpoons, or his head with fishing spears? Lay your hand on him; remember the battle—never do it again! Indeed any hope of overcoming him is false... no one is so fierce that he would dare stir him up. Who then is able to stand against

Me? Who has preceded Me that I should
pay him? Everything under heaven is
Mine" (Job 40:15-17, 41:1, 7-11).

Many scholars believe that the Behemoth and Leviathan were dinosaurs, and it seems from what we
see written here that this may well be the case. If
you read the full description I think that you will see
that it really makes sense. Whatever the case, God is
again appealing to the greatness of creation to make
His point. God is saying, "I am the Champion, the
Winner", and who can deny it? God is not egotistical;
He is just stating the truth. God is happy being God
and is not ashamed of Who He is. He wants people to
know Him, and one way to know God is through His
creation (Rom 1:18-32). He continues along these lines
for the rest of chapter forty-one.

I find it quite funny, looking at the great creation,
that skeptics would deny God made it all. If they
don't accept the God of the Bible, certainly they would
have to accept that some power beyond themselves
made all that we see. They enjoy all the good things in
creation, and do not thank God; but when bad times
come they are the first to raise their fist to God in un-
holy defiance. Here is a passage that describes how
some respond to God.

"Why do the nations rage and the people
plot vain a thing? The kings of the earth set
themselves and the rulers take counsel together, against the LORD and against His
Anointed, saying, 'Let us break their bonds

in pieces and cast away Their cords from us'" (Ps 2:1-3).

This is a picture of how people rage against God when bad things happen. Is God put off by this? Not really, listen to what He says, "He who sits in the heavens shall laugh; the Lord shall hold them in derision" (Ps 2:4). Laughter is a sign of conquest. God is totally sovereign and is unmoved by the raging of the human heart. God has emotion, but is not emotional—unlike us—He has it wrapped up tight. He understands the human plight, the good and the bad and wants Job and his friends to get the point He is trying to make.

We are getting to the climax of the story and all that has gone on up to this point is for this very reason. God wants us to get this, otherwise all that Job went through is in vain.

> "Then Job answered the Lord and said, 'I know that You can do everything, and that no purpose of Yours can be withheld from You. You asked, 'Who is this who hides counsel without knowledge?' Therefore I have uttered what I did not understand, things too wonderful for me, which I did not know. Listen, please, and let me speak; You said, I will question you and you shall answer Me. I have heard of You by the hearing of the ear, but now my eyes see You. Therefore I abhor myself and repent in dust and ashes'" (Job 42:1-6).

Here it is; not that Job didn't know that God was great before, but that all he went through caused him to see life and God differently. He was righteous before all this happened, which only comes by faith, (Abraham believed God and it was credited to him as righteousness) he was a true believer, no doubt. Now though, after Job's ordeal his eyes were opened in a greater way to see life and God more clearly. Like Jacob when he was at the Ford of the Jabbok wrestling with the Lord and finding God in a greater dimension, so Job has really found God. "I used to know You by the hearing of the ear, but now my eyes see"; this is it! When someone is truly "born again", he is spiritually *born again*, literally. This is the new birth when we see God differently. I remember when it became clear to me that Jesus was the Christ, the Son of the living God. I had heard about God all my life, but now it really made sense. This is God's world, I am His son. Not that Job was born again in Christ as we are today, but he was "born again" in the Old Testament sense. Yet he, like all who have been given rebirth, still need further understanding of God and His ways.

The story is not over, there is more.

> "And so it was, after the Lord had spoken these words to Job, that the Lord said to Eliphaz the Temanite, My wrath is aroused against you and your two friends, for you have not spoken of Me what is right, as My servant Job has" (Job 42:7).

I have wondered about God saying that Job spoke right of Him. I am thinking, "God, you just lambasted Job for his folly, and he came to the realization that he was wrong, so now you are saying he spoke right of You? How does that work?" The friends were speaking, "for God" and God didn't like it. Job was speaking out of his pain and God understood that.

When the friends spoke they did so from a self righteous perspective. It is almost like when your dog does something wrong, you know your dog; he is, for the most part, loyal and obedient. He has his days though, and when he does, you will let him know yourself. Your neighbor has no right to give your dog commands, it's your dog—your responsibility. Maybe it was like this. You don't want other people disciplining your kids. God will take care of his own; He needs no outside help, and when men speak, (like Job's friends did) they're only interfering.

Like the Israelites when the mountain was on fire. "Let Moses speak, not God." They really did not want God to speak because then they would be accountable. It would be easier to cast off Moses than God. The friends thought they were God's spokesmen and Job was arguing with them, but when God finally speaks they shut up and listen. God is upset with the friends and tells them to,

> "...take for yourselves seven bulls and seven rams, go to My servant Job, and offer up for yourselves a burnt offering, and My servant Job will pray for you. For I will accept him, lest I deal with you according to

your folly; because you have not spoken of me what is right as my servant Job has. So Eliphaz the Temanite and Bildad the Shuhite and Zophar the Naamathite went and did as the Lord commanded them, for the Lord had accepted Job. And the Lord restored Job's losses when he prayed for his friends. Indeed the Lord gave Job twice as much as he had before" (Job 42:8-10).

When God weighed in and trumped everything the friends said, we see that all of their theology was false; yet they had spoken it with great gusto. You see, they had taken God-inspired Scriptural truths and spuriously applied them, which turned them into false doctrine. That is why I said in the beginning to watch what they said, realizing that it would be suspect in the end. We need to be careful to study and apply Biblical text as a whole; within the context it is found. So to those who quote Job's friends to people who are suffering, I believe God would say the same thing, "You're not speaking of me what is right" (paraphrased). Unfortunately this happens all too often—especially in Pentecostal and Charismatic circles.

Job is not to be bitter toward them, he is to pray for them. Jesus said the same, "You have heard that it was said, you shall love you neighbor and hate your enemy. But I say to you, love your enemies, bless those who curse you, do good to those who hate you, and pray for those who spitefully use you and persecute you" (Matt 5:43-44). When he did what God said, his losses were restored. All his siblings came to him to comfort him, God increased his wealth and he made another family, with seven sons, and three exceptional daughters.

> "In all the land were found no women so beautiful as the daughters of Job; and their father gave them an inheritance among their brothers. [So they must have been wise and financially savvy enough to handle money too.] After this Job lived one hundred and forty years and saw his children and grandchildren for four generations. So Job died, old and full of days" (Job 42:15-17).

God loves a happy ending and this story proves it. But again, we have to keep the big picture in mind, which is eternity. That will be the ultimate happy ending for all who believe. We can still believe for God to help us here and now, but if things don't pan out like we think they should, we can rest assured that we will gain in the next life.

Chapter 9

Prayer and Faith

We've covered so much, and there is still more to be said. More questions come to mind that still seek answers. It comes back to this very question, "Do we live in a random universe or does God have His hand on things? ...And if He does, at what level? It seems to me from the stories we talked about that God is intimately a part of the world He created and the people in it. I want to expand on some thoughts I have touched on earlier concerning the issue of evil and suffering from a book that I read recently, *Is God to Blame?* by Gregory A. Boyd. In the book he argues against what he calls the "blueprint worldview" approach to this subject. This position says that God is in control of everything and that everything that happens is God's will.

> "The assumption that there is a specific divine reason for everything that takes place has been taught by some of the church's chief theologians. For example, Augustine of Hippo, perhaps the most influential theologian in church history, wrote: 'The

cause of things, ...which makes but is not made, is God.' And again, the will of the omnipotent is always undefeated. Many theologians believe this means that nothing ever thwarts the will of God. On this interpretation, even the most horrendous events and most evil deeds are in line with God's sovereign will".

When we read this it causes various questions to arise in us. Is God really behind the Holocaust, all the wars throughout history, the untold deaths by aids, cancer, heart disease? What about all the aborted babies and people who are in pain every day, trying to survive in abject poverty? Is this God's will? Thou shall not kill (murder) is the will of God. That is what God said along with the rest of the Ten Commandments. Why would God not operate according to what He Himself wrote? Most people accept that He would.

Many times when finding answers or just a sense of direction about what is really true, the answers are really not out at the extremes. If you have a continuum, and at one end is the "blueprint worldview" and at the other end is the "all is random worldview," the answer is not one or the other—rather it is somewhere in the middle. Not that truth is not absolute, because it is, but in these circumstances there are more questions to be asked and more variables to consider. Boyd goes on concerning what Augustine said,

"Augustine at one point encouraged Christians who had been victimized by others to find consolation in the knowledge that the perpetrators could not have harmed them unless God empowered the perpetrators and allowed them to do it for a greater good".

Without going into this in great detail, this in a nutshell, is the position of the "blueprint" model. Many have accepted this view throughout the years; it is viable, and you can make a scriptural argument for this position.

If you take this view to the extreme, prayer has little effect and therefore the element of interceding to God is not a consideration in the mix. Boyd does not go to this extreme, but argues for a more random universe. He even binds God to His own creation, saying at various points that God can't do certain things, (which I do not accept). But he does share some points on prayer that I believe will be helpful to balance out some things I've talked about up to this point. "Scripture teaches that God created a world in which He has significantly bound Himself to the prayers of His people". He uses this example,

"'The people of the land have practiced extortion and committed robbery; they have oppressed the poor and needy, and have extorted from the aliens without redress. And I sought for anyone among them who would repair the wall and stand in the breach before me on behalf of the land, so that I would not destroy it; but I found no one. Therefore I have poured out my indignation upon them' (Ez 22:29-31)".

He goes on,

"It is clear from this passage that God didn't want to judge His people despite their unjust practices. Thus He sought for someone to prevent it...most believe that standing in the breach refers to, or at least includes, intercessory prayer. After all, Scripture is full of examples of individuals and groups changing God's plan to judge people through intercessory prayer (Num 11:1-2; 14:12-20; 16:20-35; Deut 9:13-14, 18-20, 25; 2 Sam 24:17-25; 1 Kings 21:27-29; 2 Chron 12:5-8; Jer 26:19) ...Therefore the Lord said He would destroy the Israelites—had not Moses, his chosen one, stood in the breach before Him, to turn away His wrath form destroying them (Ps 106:23)".

It is clear from scripture that God does respond to prayer, He calls for it and then He responds to it. So what follows is nine points made by Boyd concerning prayer.

"There is another rarely noticed but extremely important reason why we often

144

can't know why prayer isn't answered. While prayer itself is as simple as talking to a friend, the actual mechanics of prayer are remarkably complex. Scripture hints at a number of variables that affect the impact prayer has on the world...1. God's will...I have argued against appealing to God's will as the only explanation for why prayer is or isn't answered. Yet God's will is the most basic variable affecting whether prayer is answered...(1 John 5:14, Jas 4:3)... Jesus' request for the Father to find a plan other than the cross couldn't be granted because it wasn't the Father's will. (Matt 26:39) Paul's request that his thorn in the flesh be removed was not granted...(2 Cor 12:7-10) We must be careful not to conclude that because God willed something, it is part of His perfect plan. Even with this qualification, however, we must be even more careful not to generalize Jesus' or Paul's experience to the point of concluding that every instance of suffering and every unanswered prayer are part of God's accommodating will. There are a number of variables influencing the outcome of prayer".

The second reason Boyd lists for prayer not being answered is the faith of the person being prayed for. He references Mark 6:5-6, "He could do no deed of power there, except that He laid His hands on a few sick people and cured them. And He was amazed at their unbelief." Jesus was amazed by unbelief. Being in "faith" circles all my life this passage is stressed a lot. It is good to encourage belief and true faith in Jesus as the ultimate healer. But the good thing can become a bad thing. How? By making this the only criteria for a person not being healed or receiving an answer to prayer. He echoes the same concern,

> "Here too a word of caution is in order. Some, recognizing that God's ideal will is to heal people, have concluded that whenever someone is not healed or a prayer is not answered it's because the person being prayed for lacked faith. We must not generalize to the point of making this principle the explanation for why prayer is or isn't answered".

I agree. Faith is not to be used as a club, "Your prayer wasn't answered, so you don't have faith." Faith is a catalyst to receive from God what we are asking for. Yes, Jesus did rebuke a lack of faith, but to say that this is the only reason for unanswered prayer is a mistake. If my son asks me for something and I have the power to give it to him, (not more than twenty dollars—joke) I may delay giving it to him just to see if he really wants/needs it. But I don't doubt his faith, he knows me—that I love him and have his best interests at heart. I don't wait to see if he believes it enough. God wants us to believe and is honored when we do, but the accuser of the brethren (Rev 12:10) stands to condemn you if you do not receive the answer, accusing you for not having enough faith. More could be said here but I will refrain.

The next reason for unanswered prayer, according to Boyd, is the faith of people who are praying for others. This is something I put to people who say I don't have enough faith for my healing miracle. I say jokingly, "Maybe it's your lack of faith that's the reason for me not being healed; maybe it is you—not me." In Luke 5:20 the friends' faith caused them to lower their paralyzed friend to Jesus, where he was healed. Same with the Roman centurion, (Matt 8:13) it was his faith that caused Jesus to say, "Go; let it be done for you according to your faith." It was his faith—not the boy's—that brought the healing.

> "The principle here is that the strength of our faith in praying for another person increases the power of our prayer. James taught that we must 'Ask in faith, never doubting, for the one who doubts is like the wave of the sea, driven and tossed by the wind; for the doubter, being double minded and unstable in every way, must not expect to receive anything from the Lord' (James 1:6-7)".

Boyd goes on,

"Again, we must avoid reducing this principle to a simplistic formula that explains
all instances of unanswered prayer. Whenever we turn principles into formulas, we
end up either indicting God or other people. Reality is always more complex than
formulas".

There is often more than just one reason for prayer
not being answered.

The forth reason is a lack of persistence. As I just
said about my son, sometimes we don't know what
we really want, but when we persist in pursuing
something, it's a very good indication that we really
do want that thing. This is a principle of life, you see it
in every successful person or business; the idea of not
giving up. Luke 18:1-8 is the story of the widow and
the unjust judge.

"Then He spoke a parable to them, that
men always ought to pray and not lose
heart, saying, 'There was in a certain city a
judge who did not fear God or regard man.
Now there was a widow in that city, and
she came to him, saying, get justice for me
from my adversary. And he would not for
a while; but afterward he said within himself, though I do not fear God nor regard
man, yet because this widow troubles me I

will avenge her, lest by her continual coming she weary me.' Then the Lord said,
'Hear what the unjust judge said. And
shall God not avenge His own elect who
cry out day and night to Him, though he
bears long with them? I tell you that He
will avenge them speedily, nevertheless
when the Son of Man comes, will He really
find faith on the earth?'"

It seems from this passage that faith and persistence go hand in hand. You cannot divorce faith from
persistence, and this is what is common among the
more faith-centered churches. They often mistakenly
look at faith as a one shot deal. The focus is drum-
ming up enough faith to get the results we seek right
now, instead of teaching that faith is activated over the
long haul, as we have seen in the stories of Jacob, Joseph, David and Job.

"Again we must be careful to avoid simplistic, formulaic over-generalizations. Jesus' teaching on the need for persistence
doesn't mean that whenever a prayer isn't
answered it's because we didn't pray long
enough...it does mean, though, that when a
matter of prayer is on our heart, we should
be persistent about it".

"Fifth is the amount of people praying: corporate prayer. There are many instances
of this in the Bible, (Neh 9:1; 2 Chron 7:14;

Matt 26:36, 41; Acts 1:13-14; 4:24-30; Eph 6:19-20; Col 4:3-4; 1 Thess 5:25, 2 Thess 3:1; Heb 13:18; Jas 5:13-16)".

We all need help sometimes in our exasperation at praying. Sometimes we feel like we are hitting a brick wall by ourselves so we have to summon the troops. Jesus said, "If two of you agree on earth about anything you ask, it will be done for you by my Father in heaven. For where two or three are gathered in my name, I am there among them" (Matt 18:19-20). I have been blessed through the years to have prayer partners who have been able to agree with me for things. When there are two agreeing about a thing there is more of a likelihood that that thing is indeed something that is acceptable. Let's face it, we all get into more self-centered prayers, but when we pray in agreement with someone, if the other person's heart does not feel the "amen" in it, it is unlikely that the prayer will be answered. This is not to say that our individual prayers are not sincere or valid. Jesus said individual prayers are just as effective. (Matt 21:22; Mk 11:24; Jn 14:13-14; 15:7, 16) So both individual and corporate prayer is effective, but that is not to say that if these prayers are not answered it is because of a lack of numbers in prayer. For, "no individual or group always has prayers answered exactly as requested" (140).

Sixth: human free will. This one intrigues me greatly; I know that this matter of free will is very controversial. The world that God made incorporates this matter of will, our will. The garden is where this will is first seen on the human level. God gave Adam and Eve a choice and a warning if they made the wrong choice.

> "Then the Lord God took the man and put him in the Garden of Eden to tend and keep it. And the Lord God commanded the man saying, 'Of every tree in the garden you may freely eat; but of the tree of the knowledge of good and evil you shall not eat, for in the day that you shall eat of it you shall surly die" (Gen 2:15-17).

This is the greatest gift that God has given the human family in my estimation. Without it we are simply robots responding the way we are programmed. There can be no real love if there is no real freedom.

Freedom is a gift—but love is a decision. Love is a choice. To obey is a choice, and love and obedience are interconnected. You can obey without love, (1 Cor 13) but you really cannot love without obedience. Love and adultery, stealing and keeping your hands off other people's stuff, lying and telling the truth, these are opposites. You can't truthfully love someone and steal from them. Here is one that most people have a problem with. You cannot love your wife and commit adultery. You may repent if you have done this and reconnect in love, (if that is possible) but the act of adultery and love are incongruent. We could go deep into the sin nature and its affects on us—that would be another book—but for the sake of this subject let's admit that wrongdoing and love do not mix. "In the day that you shall eat in that day you shall surly die" (Gen 2:17). When Adam and Eve ate, death came upon the human family. But on that day God's plan for our way out was also set in motion. "'And I will put enmity between you and the woman, and between your seed and her Seed; He shall bruise your head, and you shall bruise His heal,' God said to Satan" (Gen 3:15).

So for all those who think the punishment was too great, (and I have, and do at times) we cannot forget that God promised a Redeemer to come and reverse the curse. That is what Jesus did and does; He is God's love in action. So human will is in the mix of life and sad to say, people make wrong choices, and as a result innocent people suffer. (The Holocaust and many other genocides throughout history, child abuse, those like me, whose lives have been torn apart by drunk drivers, etc.) God respects a man's right to make a choice, "In fact, Hell is a testimony to how seriously God takes free will".

Boyd continues,

"In a similar fashion God works primarily by influencing us at a level of our innermost being. By His own design his influence in a person's life is intensified when His people pray for that person...He will not undermine a person's say-so by controlling him or her, regardless of how much we pray...God will not...simply turn people into robots to answer our prayers".

The seventh reason for unanswered prayer is one you don't hear much about: angelic free will.

"Human beings are not the only agents in the cosmos who possess morally responsible say-so. Spirit agents (referred to in Scripture as angels, gods, demons, principles, powers, authorities, rulers) also possess free will. Their activity is another variable that influences prayer".

There is an unseen world that is described in the Bible that is full of all these agents, the good and the bad. Daniel 10:12-13 talks about how Daniel was praying and fasting and God dispatched an angel in response to his prayer. The angel, however, was met with resistance from the prince of Persia and was delayed.

"Often when prayers (and plans) don't bring about the outcome we hoped, people say something like, God's timing is the right timing. But this is too simplistic. The delay Daniel experienced had nothing to do with God's timing but with interference in the spiritual realm".

It could be said that all this "interference" was a part of God's will, but the point is well taken. Paul was, "thwarted" by Satan

(1 Thess 2:17-18) Boyd notes writer Walter Wink who,

"…notes that at least in some circumstances, principalities and powers are able to hold the Lord at bay. From this he concludes that prayer involves not just God and people, but God and the powers. What God is able to do in the world is hindered, to a considerable extent, by the rebelliousness, resistance and self interest of the Powers exercising their freedom under God".

I often think about the analogy that I talked about in the beginning concerning the *Raiders of the Lost Ark*. The enemy is wielding a machete threatening Indiana Jones. He looks at the man and simply pulls out a gun and shoots him. The mystery in all this is why doesn't God just "shoot" all his enemies? He has enlisted us in the battle, yes, He could and soon will, put all His enemies under His feet, (Rom 16:20) but for now we must be aware of these powers and pray. "All prayer that furthers God's will on earth confronts spiritual powers that resist God's will from being accomplished on earth".

This brings us to the next logical point, number eight: the number and strength of spirit agents. Boyd speaks about various passages that indicate that the amount of forces have a lot to do with how the battle goes in prayer.

"As Jesus continued His teaching, he touched on the significance of the number

> of opposition forces. If a person who has
> had an unclean spirit cast out isn't careful,
> the spirit may eventually return with sev-
> en spirits more evil that itself and take up
> residence in this person once again. ..we
> see the that the greater number of spirit
> agents we are up against, the worse situa-
> tion we're in".

The amount of spirits is an issue for sure, but we have to remember as New Testament believers that we are possessed by God's Spirit and ultimately the greater One in us is greater than anything in the world (1 John 4:4). The battle is vast and the sheer numbers of spiritual powers are beyond our human compre-hension; without God helping us by the discerning of spirits, we will in no way be able to perceive things in the right way. Our imagination will play tricks on us, and many have used their imagination to give the impression that they understand the spirit realm in a way that others don't. I really have little trust in man or his ability in this area, though I do believe in the gift of the discerning Spirits (1 Cor 12:10). We should ask God for wisdom, (James 1:5) concerning the trials we are going through so we can pray accordingly.

Probably the most common and logical reason for unanswered prayer is what most people believe, number nine: the presence of sin. Most think that if they live a good life then God "owes" them answers to prayer. Like Santa coming to reward the good and discipline the bad. If you're a good boy Santa will give you nice toys but if you're bad, you'd better watch out. I do a lot of my writing in coffee shops, which is where I am now, and since it is Christmastime, I'm hearing all about Rudolph, Santa, Jingle Bells and—oh yeah, Jesus. He is in there somewhere, I think. How did the Gift of God get confused with all these others? (Yes, I am off topic, sorry.) Anyway, though sin is an issue, like all the ones we talked about, it is not the only one. In Israel they suffered a terrible defeat and Joshua came to God and asked, "What is the problem?" The answer came, "Stand up! Why have you fallen upon your face? Israel has sinned" (Josh 7:10-11).

> "This episode illustrates the principle that in some cases God wants us to do something (e.g., repent, or confront sin) before He will hear our prayer. For example, no one would be surprised if God told an abusive husband that prayer for his wife's love is useless until he stops beating her!".

Jesus said if we do not forgive, than God will not hear us (Mk 11:25). Peter says that if you don't treat your wife right your prayers would be hindered (1 Peter 3:7). This again is very tricky, and for zealous Christians it can be misunderstood. We are all plagued with sin and various issues of our hearts, and we will never be free from sin and its influence until we leave this world. Though I have met folks who feel they are 100% free from sin and all its power. Boyd concludes,

> "Of course we must avoid the dreadful conclusion that the prayer of people with sin is useless, for we are all sinners (especially the one who claims to have no sin, (1 John 1:10))! Therefore we must not assume that a prayer wasn't answered because of sin in a person's life. Except in obvious cases—for example, an abusive husband's prayer for his wife to love him—only God can know this".

I have included these excerpts from Boyd's book because I think that in our walk of faith some of what we go through is because we don't pray as we should, but other things are totally beyond our control as in the cases of the Old Testament figures I have talked about. I don't think God wants us to bang our heads against the wall, (because it feels good when we stop—joke) to try to figure out what in the world is happening, and why we are not seeing the results we long for. I speak from personal experience. After over seven years (as of 2009) years of praying and working toward healing of my paralysis, I am getting better but not "healed" yet. I do not consider myself a perfect person (nor do my wife and kids) but I can say I have sincerely prayed during these years since the accident… (as have many God-fearing people.)

I have asked, "Why…? What…? and When…?" but I feel no closer to answers. (Sorry for the disappointment.) I wish I could say, "Oh yes, it's a, b, or c," but I cannot. Many would say I do not have faith by saying these things. They would conclude that God is punishing me or disciplining me. After this amount of time I feel I should be farther along. I feel in many ways with all the time and effort I have put into my recovery that I should be much better by now. However, I'm not where I used to be, and I am where I am only through prayer and hard work. If you're walking by faith you should be praying by faith and working by faith. That is not to say that if things are not the way you think they should be, it is a result of a lack of prayer and faith. Remember the four men I have centered on; they went through difficult challenges, and at strategic times God showed up and did what He ordained to do from the foundations of the earth. Nothing will stop God's will if we hang on in faith. We have to learn to accept where we are on the way to where we are going. We need to learn the lessons that God wants us to learn and move forward in our faith, hope and love.

Chapter 10

Faith and Hearing God Speak

When we talk about faith we have to talk about discerning God's will—or some would say His voice. This subject has been a source of confusion for many through the years. In doing research for this book, I came across a lot of good thoughts on hearing the voice of God in a book I picked up at the library a few months ago. I do not know the author personally and had never heard of the book previously, but when my eyes landed on it my initial thought was, "I have to read this." The book is called *God Talk* by Ruth A. Tucker. It's about trying to hear God's voice and discerning His will; she talks about the use and abuse in this matter and references several other authors and speakers. With all the talk about faith, we have to talk about hearing the voice of God because, "faith comes by hearing and hearing by the word of God" (Rom 10:17). For some this means hearing the scriptures taught in proper context, and then the proper application made. For others it means hearing a direct word from God, a "rhema" word that is specific to them and their situation. The Logos is the written word, and the Rhema is the one that leaps out off the page and connects with the heart, bringing freedom and release. For those who are very zealous for God and to know His will this "rhema word" theology has been a real source of blessing, but for others—a source of confusion.

Tucker talks about Joyce Huggett, a woman who was zealous to hear the voice of God and some of the conclusions she came up with.

> "So what does the Bible actually have to say about listening to the voice of God? This is a question that has troubled many Christians through the centuries. For Joyce Huggett, the matter created conflict with her husband, who insisted the Bible alone was sufficient. 'Trapped between this teaching, the anxiety of my friends and an irresistible thirst to know more about listening to God,' she writes, 'there seemed only one way forward. I would have to search the Bible for myself to see whether it describes the kind of listening to God which had struck a cord within my heart'".

Tucker responds to some of the information that Huggett got, which was that God does breakthrough and speak. She listed numerous passages, some of which focused on the Shepard and the sheep (John 10:14-16). The sheep know the Shepard's voice. This is one aspect of hearing God that she came up with.

"...sheep do not have to move into mode of meditation to hear the Shepard's voice. Rather they hear it while they are doing what they do—graze. Secondly, their listening is not a matter of comprehending but simply recognizing the voice and the presence of the master. In her listening, Huggett was receiving messages that were unique for her. No single sheep has such access to the shepherd".

This is a good point. It seems that Huggett was receiving unique messages to her but God is interested in the whole flock. If He does speak to an individual sheep it is for the whole flock to benefit from as well. I believe in prophetic words, (these are statements that supposedly come directly from God to a person or church) but I have to say I have only seen it operate in what I felt was a true gift a few times. I have seen much abuse, "God said, God told me..." This becomes the benchmark, and rather than sensing the direction of God through the Holy Spirit and sound wisdom, direction is based on this outside "voice" of God. Huggett seems to have come to this conclusion:

"Despite her Bible study and her longing to hear God's voice, Huggett very honestly admitted after an intense period of contemplative prayer that hearing the voice of God is more difficult than she first imagined. She concedes that many mistakes are made in discerning whether the voice

is God's, her own or the devil's. 'For the
next twelve months I became more cau-
tious about listening to the voice of God,'
she writes, 'I now realize that we can never
be one hundred percent certain that the
picture we see or the voice we hear or the
prophecy we speak out is winged to us
from God'".

This woman went down the road, maybe not the
total "faith" road, the one paved by Kenneth Hagin or
Kenneth Copland, but she inquired of the Lord and
studied His word. She made some valid conclusions
to which Tucker responds,

"Huggett's honesty is refreshing; she recognizes that the voice of God is elusive. It
certainly was for the Old Testament prophets. Habakkuk presents an answer from
God, but only after he has written in the
opening lines, 'How long, O Lord, must I
call for help, but you do not listen?' (Hab
1:2). Jeremiah mirrors this refrain, He can
confidently proclaim, 'This is what the
Lord Almighty says', but he too suffers
from God's silence—and God's rejection".

I wrote my senior paper on "Hearing the Voice of
God." My main point was that if you are practicing
Romans 12:1-2, submitting yourself to God and not
being conformed to the world, you could hear the
Lord speak. I do believe that we should practice what

is written in the Bible first and foremost. There is no reason to want to ride a motorcycle if you can't ride a bicycle. You have to get through first grade to get to second. There is a process of growth in grace and knowledge of the Lord and His will, so in order to hear from God, make sure you're submitting to Him first. Jacob worked for Laban twenty years and there is no reference of him hearing God during that time. He heard God speak at strategic times for a specific purpose. Job complained to his friends about all the hell that he was going through and it was not until the end of the book that God spoke. David did not hear God for many years while running from Saul, and when he defected to the Philistines there is no record of him hearing God again for a year and four months. Joseph had dreams from God, but there is no record of him hearing God from day to day. This is where I have seen, and continue to see abuse, especially within the faith churches. The leader is the one who hears from God, and if you don't like it, leave. This can become dangerous, and many have been abused and confused by this approach.

I think we have to "do justly, love mercy and walk humbly with God" and really make sure it is God speaking if we believe He is. So it is not either/or but rather both/and. It is not just the written word of God, though that is foundational, first and foremost. Spring boarding from a close connection with what is written, then God may speak to us, but it may be many years until we hear from Him. In the meantime we, like Job, Jacob, David and Joseph should be faithful to what we know, trusting God to speak in His time, not manufacturing His voice or imagining we hear it when we don't. Here is another passage from Tucker's book:

"Silence for many people is unbearable. But we must continually remind ourselves that silence does not mean abandonment, nor does silence mean separation. Even as one has observed the disappearance of God in the Hebrew Bible, writes Friedman, [a writer whom Tucker quotes] one is left with the observation that this tapestry of divine-human acquaintance and divine-human balance and divine-human struggle also includes the possibility of a divine-human reunion. That divine-human reunion is demonstrated most profoundly in the resurrection...we live essentially in the silence of God. But there is for the Christian, that whispering hope made possible through the death of Christ on the cross—a cross that led to the tomb and three days of what must have seemed like unbearable silence for the Son of Man...we share in the suffering of the silence that followed, especially in those moments when we feel most abandoned by God. But for us there is a comforting voice of Jesus who knows our suffering—albeit a voice that is sometimes smothered amidst our pain. This is not a voice per se but a whisper of hope, breathing a lesson unheard".

Whatever you believe about where Jesus went after He died, the silence that was a part of the disciples' life after his death was real. Jesus experienced separation from God on the cross, "Why have you forsaken Me?" Not just silence but total separation. So there was silence on many fronts, for Jesus and the disciples, but this quiet had a purpose, it was not a sign of rejection at all. I know that many of you may still be struggling with many things you have seen and heard about God and the church. Some of you are in, or have come out of abusive churches with power- and money-hungry pastors who do not care for the flock. It may have seemed right in the beginning but now you have doubts. Additionally you may not seem to be hearing clearly from God in your personal life. You may be in physical or emotional pain, feeling and believing that God is gone—if He ever was with you. I want to encourage you. God has not left you. Call on Him; He will lift you up. Wait on Him, learn from these men, and know that true faith is in for the long haul. If you are in a "dry" time, trust that it's for a reason. As I said, after over seven years in this paralyzed condition my doubts have been very strong. I have been through Bible College and Seminary but they do not prepare you for this. When I hear of people bringing God's word into question I totally understand. Before I would have been less patient, but now I get it. There are things in the Bible that are hard to understand, (2 Peter 3:16) and in our pain and anguish we are tempted to distort the clear message of the Bible. Paul said though, "...that if Christ is not risen, your faith is futile, you are still in your sins...if the dead do not rise, let us eat and drink, for tomorrow we die" (1 Cor 15:17, 32b).

And this is the central theme of the Word of God, John 3:16, "For God so loved the world, He gave His only begotten Son that whosoever believes in Him should not perish but have everlasting life." This historical truth is assaulted, now as it has been through the ages, mainly due to people not understanding that suffering and love are not mutually exclusive. If God is love, then why all the suffering? The Gospel trumps the suffering argument. God *is* love and *does* allow suffering. He allowed His Son to suffer—to save us—from the foundations of the world (Rev 13:8). The devil plays this doubt card all the time but God always counters it with this very truth. We cannot fully explain this mystery of suffering and pain, nor can we fully comprehend the vast love of God to do that for you and me. It is mind blowing.

This brings us back again to what God's will is for us; and this is very tricky because we subconsciously think that God's will is always bigger and better. A cross, a prison, a remote island—this can't be God's will. A better paying career, a bigger ministry, a better house or car, yes—this is God's will. I confess I struggle with these thoughts, especially in the circles I hang around in. Faith and more stuff go hand in hand; of course God wants better for you. And I do think He does, generally. David prayed, "May the Lord give you increase more and more, you and your children. May you be blessed by the Lord, who made heaven and earth" (Ps 115:14-15). Jacob increased, Joseph increased, David increased and Job increased. In the New Testament though, you do not get this emphasis in terms of stuff and money. The thought is that Christ and the Apostles were generally poor in capital but rich in God's Spirit. I like the verse in Psalms, "Do not trust in oppression, nor vainly hope in robbery; if riches increase, do not set your heart upon them" (Ps 112:10). In other words, it's not a blanket statement that faith and increased money are intertwined.

We have Americanized this to the point of absurdity. Note these statements concerning God's call to preach in *God Talk*:

> "In reflecting on the pastoral call, Peterson [another writer quoted by Tucker] speaks with insight on God's presence and absence, and how that can effect one's attitude and behavior. 'Ironies abound in the pastoral vocation,' he writes, 'Jonah uses the command of the Lord to avoid the presence of the Lord. Lest we miss the irony, the phrase Tarshish, [meaning] away from the presence of the Lord, occurs twice in one verse.' Then he asks: 'Why would anyone, who has known God's voice, flee from His presence?' ...It happens in ministry. I flee the face of God for a world of religion, where I can manipulate people and acquire godlike attributes to myself. The moment I entertain the possibility of glory for myself, I want to blot out the face of the

Lord and seek a place where I can develop my power. Anyone can be so tempted, but pastors have the temptation compounded because we have a constituency with which to act godlike. Unlike other temptations, this one easily escapes detection, passing itself off as virtue".

Good pastors feed the flock with God's word. They stand for truth and in the gap on behalf of the "land" which is the people. Unlike the world system of business or religion, a true man of God seeks not promotion, (whatever that is to you) but faithfulness in God's service. Paul said, "Therefore, my beloved brethren, be steadfast, immovable, always abounding in the work of the Lord, knowing that your labor is not in vain in the Lord" (1 Cor 15:8). But in our human-ness we often go astray from this model and fall into the trap of self advancement. It is not easy; if it were, everyone would be doing it!

I want to share a little more of what is written in Ruth Tucker's book.

"Claiming God as an ally in decision mak-ing, particularly when other people are involved, can be manipulative and tanta-mount to spiritual abuse when the person claiming God's sanction is in a position if spiritual authority. I recently heard the bearer of bad news introduce his decision with, 'I've spent a lot of time in prayer about this', thus implying that a judgment that was otherwise unjust was somehow sanctioned by God. This is a touchy matter. As Christians we claim to have special access to the leading of God, the leading of the Holy Spirit. But do we too easily manipulate that claim of privileged access to our own advantage? Without even thinking, we readily identify a job promotion or a pastoral promotion or a good buy on a brand new SUV or a bigger and better house as God's blessing. But how do we know that because something seems to promote our lifestyle or career that it is what God wants? We praise the Lord and thank the Lord and give testimonies of God's goodness to us, but do we ever think that maybe we are thanking and praising the Lord for things that have little to do with God's will for our lives? Too often we pray for something—admission in the Ivy League university, for example—then get what we pray for, we automatically assume the answer to prayer is God's blessing or God's will. Prayer and the desire for the will of God are bound up with very subjective feelings and motives. It is presumptuous to assume that our aspirations are necessarily the same as God's".

If Jacob knew what was in store at Uncle Laban's house I wonder if he would have gone. He could have reasoned many different directions and gone a different way. Even though he came out with a family and a lot of stuff in the end, he could have got all that without the hassle of uncle Laban. Job did not see his situation as God's will, but look at the comfort we have derived from his life. He stated, "Though He slay me, yet will I trust Him. Even so, I will defend my ways before Him" (Job 13:15). The point is, that in your walk of faith, you cannot compare where you are now with where you think you should be or where others are, or how many material things you have. This will not help you. Humble yourself under the mighty hand of God...He will lift you up (James 4:10).

Some people will say that all this is too technical, lighten up; it's not all that complicated. But is that true? What is the purpose of this life? To gain acceptance with "big" people, to gain money, fame etc? For many these things are first and foremost, but for those who claim to be Christians, the seeking of these should be secondary at best. David was exasperated by life and the battles he was involved in and was wondering about God's will when he said,

> "Teach me Your way, O Lord, and lead me in a smooth path, because of my enemies. Do not deliver me to the will of my adversaries, for false witnesses have risen against me. And such as breathe out violence. I would have lost heart, unless I believed I would see the goodness of the Lord in the land of the living" (Ps 27:11-13).

Life is sometimes hard and it is important in those times to believe that we will in fact see the goodness of the Lord in the land of the living. You will see it when you hold on in faith. Many do not wait on God, then become discouraged and miss seeing the hand of God moving in their circumstances. He finishes this prayer with these words, "Wait on the Lord and be of good courage, and He shall strengthen your heart. Wait I say on the Lord" (Ps 27:14).

This is a far cry from what many accept as God's way of dealing and speaking to us. I refer again to the book *God Talk*. Tucker notes Agnes Sanford, another speaker/writer:

> "Agnes Sanford once heard the Spirit tell her not to board a certain airplane. She did not and the plane crashed. Later, when she told this story to a group, one woman rather angrily asked her why God would speak to her and not to others. Agnes immediately replied, 'Oh, I think He was speaking to all of us...But only a few listen'".

To this Tucker responds, "That God singled out Sanford to escape a plane crash because she was listening and punished others with death because they were not is an arrogant claim".

This is what I believe is appalling to God. The Old Testament prophets could boldly claim, "Thus says the Lord" and be 100% right. These were special people with a special calling, set apart for God to do and say what God wanted. None of us today has this, (sorry Benny Hinn and Kenneth Copeland) and those who claim to have often been found out to be wrong. These men may have gifts of wisdom and knowledge but when they add to God's word and give people false hope, they themselves are false prophets. The Bible says we should not revere them.

She goes on,

> "There is only one way, it seems to me, to respond to such circumstances. Rather than claiming that God saved me while letting all the others perish, I should humbly thank God for the gift of life and rededicate myself to God in service to others".

This is opposite of the "look at me, I am healthy and wealthy, saved from all harm," attitude that is haughty at best.

> "There is a downside to the creeping subjectivist that is so prevalent in contemporary Christianity, whether it emerges in sets of rules and steps and principles of sample case studies. It's all too easy to make presumptuous claims of having a special message from God—especially if a voice is brought forth through the right techniques and methods. Does God speak only at our beck and call? Does God speak only when we appropriate a novel system or twelve step program?".

I have seen the destruction of the "God told me" mindset. People have married the wrong people, accepted the wrong jobs, gone in the wrong direction and literally have lost what could have been an effective ministry because they thought God was telling them a particular thing. When that thing was acted on it brought destruction not blessing. It happens with building projects that preachers feel "led" to embark on and later learn they are over their heads. But, "God told me" and who can argue with that? Hey, if God told you, who am I to stand in your way? It becomes the blanket statement for everything. Many times it is a bad deal.

However, we are not going to throw the baby out with the bath water. God does speak and we can hear. I remember when I was at college, talk of hearing God and doing His will were commonplace. I would go for long walks in the woods asking God to speak to me. There was a spring break coming up and after reading the many stories of missionaries and open air speakers I sought to go to Florida to preach to spring breakers. But I was very troubled by my inability to really hear from God. My Pastor at the time had a cabin in the woods, in the foothills of the Smoky Mountains. I love Georgia; it is such a rich state with great hills and woods. So, rather than go to Florida, I went to Pastor George's cabin. It was tucked in the woods with trees and brush all around. In fact there were acres and acres of woods all around the cabin. I determined that I would go and hear God speak to me. I brought nothing but water and juice. The first night I laid on a bench outside the cabin, I said, here is my body, a living sacrifice (Rom 12:1-2). I felt the presence of God very strongly.

About the third day I went for a walk and got totally lost. I mean I had no idea where I was. It was later in the afternoon and I had no matches for a fire. I figured this would be a good time hear the voice of God, so I said, "God speak to me, I am lost." I do not want to over dramatize this but I honestly felt God tell me to go this way or go that way. Right before nightfall I came to a paved road, got my bearings and walked back to the cabin. I know this sounds purely subjective, but it really did happen. I can't say that I have ever heard God in the same way since that day, but I have never been in the same situation either.

About the last day that I was there I looked up to the sky. I saw a hawk flying high above me, he was not flapping his wings frantically, but using the wind to gracefully soar. Again, this is subjective but I sensed God tell me, "Do you see that hawk? That is how I want you to be, at rest, soaring on the wind. Do not be anxious, spread your wings and fly with Me." I have always struggled with being anxious, always wondering what I should do, where I should go, what God wanted me to do, etc. So this was a true blessing and whenever I am tempted to be anxious and fret, I recall the hawk. Every time I see one my spirit rises within me; there is my teacher. Lord help me to be like the hawk, soaring on the wind of Your Spirit.

Amazingly, God does speak through His creation. He asked Job about the animals, the Behemoth and the

Leviathan. He wanted Job to recall these great cre-
ations and learn. I do think we can gain many things
looking and observing creation and all it has to teach
us. Maybe we shouldn't go as far as St. Francis, (the
famous Catholic Monk) who used to preach to the
birds, but we can gain a lot from observing the work
of His hands (Ps 19:1). When I was lost in the woods,
I felt God speak to my inner man. I was in a tough
place so I think God was having mercy on me. But
when I saw the hawk I was in a more relaxed state.
My point is that God speaks through many means at
various times. More people can relate to an eagle or
a hawk and make an application to their life versus
hearing God speak to their heart. The latter is much
more subjective and suspect, while the former is more
objective and generally accepted.

Hearing God is a possibility, however. Tucker
writes:

> "Do we then conclude that it is impossible
> to hear the voice of God? We should not
> dismiss the concept of listening altogether,
> but we need a humility in our claims of
> hearing God's voice. Fredrick Buechner
> [preacher/writer] counsels his readers that
> the time may come when we need to stop
> speaking and thinking and reading and
> start watching and listening—which he
> confesses is difficult for him because he is
> an addicted speaker, thinker, reader. His
> concept of prayer is primarily that of lis-

tening to God: prayer not as speaking to
God, which in a scattered way I do many
times a day because I cannot help doing it,
but prayer as being deeply silent, as watching and listening for God to speak...What
deadens us most to God's presence within
us, I think, is the inner duologue that we are
continuously engaged in with ourselves,
the endless chatter of human thought. I
suspect that there is nothing more crucial
to true spiritual comfort...than being able
from time to time to stop that chatter including the chatter of spoken prayer. If we
choose to seek the silence of the holy place,
or to open ourselves to it's seeking, I think
there is no surer way than by keeping silent".

There is no sure "method" for hearing God. All the
men discussed earlier heard God in different ways at
different times. Throughout the New Testament the
Apostles heard God speak in various ways in various circumstances, and the purpose was always to
promote the Kingdom message. I referred in my last
book, *Walking This Walk*, about a man I used to work
with. I worked for a season for a concrete company,
driving transit mix trucks, (the heavy-duty ones with
the big spinning barrels on them.) In the trucks are
radios (sometimes they worked sometimes not) for us
to communicate back to dispatch what was going on
or if we needed anything. Obviously, we were not to

be talking small talk or anything that did not directly relate to the concrete business, however, if we were in trouble we could radio in and (hopefully) get a response. One day a driver flipped his truck over and was (thankfully) able to use the radio to transmit a message…probably something like, "Help!"

The point is that we could talk to "base" for business reasons, and if we were in trouble. Not that we have to limit our conversation to God to these two things but let's face it, we who are true disciples of Jesus are on a mission and we need to communicate with God all the time about His business and about everything else. If we need help, He will send it. Like everything else in life, we learn more by doing than anything else. We listen to God the same way we listen to anyone else; we talk to Him the same way. Today there are many distractions, things that make it harder to hear the voice of God. We have many responsibilities and various trials that cause us to become sidetracked and discouraged, not spending the time to quietly listen—but we can press in, wait on Him, and find the comfort of His voice.

Chapter 11

Faith, Disappointment and Anger

Two questions arise when we think about our relationship with God, number one: Is it right to be angry at God? And two: What about God's silence, is that a sign of His rejection of me? The first question has been talked about by theologians for centuries. Some say it is wrong to be angry with God no matter what; it is a show of unbelief. The other camp says it is totally natural to be angry with God when we see the injustices of life to us and others. Which is right? In the first position Ruth Tucker writes,

> "The book of Job stands as an everlasting
> monument to God's acceptance of anger—
> over and above, I would argue, apologetic
> arguments to explain away the problem of
> pain. The story of Job is a universal story
> that serves as a backdrop for our personal
> accounts of pain and suffering".

On the other side author and Pastor John Piper, (whom I like) says in *Suffering and the Sovereignty of God* that it is wrong to be angry with God. "It is never,

ever, ever, right to be angry with God...If a person sins by being angry with God, that person should surely confess the sin, any anger against God is absolutely wrong" (140). He sites Jonah being angry at God for having mercy on the city. God rebuked him in the end for it. "Then the Lord said, Is it right for you to be angry?" (Jonah 4:4). Some may argue that God was confronting Jonah's unjust anger and that this is different from Job and his anger over his situation. At the end of the book of Job God says, "And so it was, after the Lord had spoken these words to Job, that the Lord said to Eliphaz the Temanite, My wrath is aroused against you and your two friends, for you have not spoken of Me what is right, as my servant Job has" (Job 42:8). That is quite a statement coming from God about Job. Job expressed anger in many ways but God never singled him out and said, "Your anger was sin." In the book of James, he says, "For the wrath of man does not produce the righteousness of God" (James 1:20). Paul says, "Be angry, and do not sin, do not let the sun go down on your wrath" (Eph 4:26). God knows we will be angry at Him, other people, ourselves, the situation. At the end of the day though, it is our faith that will release all of our emotions to the power and presence of God. To be human is not a sin and being angry is a part of being human.

The silence of God is a wonder, to be sure. I know when my kids are hurting and there is something that I could say that would help them it is hard for me to not say anything. But God is not like me or you. He knows us better than we know ourselves, and when I think of it, my kids rarely listen to me anyway unless they are totally desperate. (Teenagers know it all, you know.) I think God treats us the same way and takes our receptiveness into consideration to a certain extent. He will speak when we are ready to listen. After all that Job went through—losing his family and health and having to listen to his "friends" advice and condemnation—God then spoke at the end. I do not agree that God is everlastingly silent; I think He knows when to speak. He knows when we will truly listen. It took seven years of "grazing" in the field until Nebuchadnezzar finally looked up to heaven to receive God's help (Dan 4:31-35). When God is silent we should not be afraid of it, rather we should remind ourselves of all He has said in His word, take it and apply it to our lives. Never let human emotions keep you away from God. Remember that condemnation is a killer. (Condemnation is the feeling that we are guilty even though we have done no wrong, which differs from conviction, where we feel remorseful, but hopeful that we can do better next time.) Many times it's condemnation that we struggle with, and this is often based on our emotions not lining up with what we feel is "Christian."

Dr. Timothy Johnson, the ABC medical journalist, makes a statement in his book *Finding God in the Questions*, concerning the "stars" and "servants" of our day; the stars being the actors, athletes and musicians; the servants being doctors, nurses and anyone else who wants to help humanity in significant ways. He says that though he benefits from the accolades of his peers for a job well done, it is more satisfying to him to help common people. With our emphasis being a walk of faith and what that really is, I want to quote what he says about a person who is struggling with walking with Jesus.

> "I just can't do it. I am so far away from meeting that standard that I might as well not even try. That is also the truth: although we may believe that the way of Jesus is the most healthy and whole way of life, we also know that none of us is capable of living that way with any degree of regularity. Where does that leave us? Obviously, I have no easy answers—meaning answers that are easy to incorporate into our daily lives. And I cringe at television preachers and book writers who suggest that if you simply follow Jesus, you will be led to a path of comfort and ease and even financial reward".

This is so prevalent in modern Christian thought and teaching. In many ways the "cure" is worse than the disease because it is only temporary and thus impotent. Some preachers give the impression that if you obey or follow God's word you will be immune to suffering. Those of us who are obedient followers who have also experienced massive quantities of pain in all its forms know how lame this teaching is.

"The truth is that Jesus never painted such a rosy picture. In fact, as I read the Gospels, the only gift He promised for sure is that if we attempted to follow His teachings, we would be closer to the heart of God than we would otherwise be--and that He Himself would be present in our lives if we attempted to do so".

Before you accuse Dr. Johnson of spouting another formula, listen to his final words on this issue.

"Now I suspect that this mention of Jesus' presence in our lives as a result of our attempt to follow his teachings and example will give some of you spiritual shivers if not outright intellectual indigestion. So let me hasten to add that I am not suggesting that if you attempt to follow Jesus, you can expect mystical magic or emotional ecstasy—though some spiritual sages through the ages have claimed such feelings. But I am saying that I deeply believe that if anyone who attempts to follow Jesus—even in tiny footsteps full of failures—will begin a journey of exploration that will lead to a deeper relationship with the God of creation than would otherwise be possible".

My conversion was dramatic in terms of external things. I stopped drinking and drugging and made a complete turn around. Not long after, I noticed that many Christians did not share my zeal. Many did not come from my same background, therefore their experience was not the same—which is common sense, right? Though at the time I assimilated some of this, deep down I questioned the truthfulness of their experience. I thought at the time that if someone was not talking Jesus twenty-four/seven that somehow their experience was suspect. Since then I have come to accept that people are people. (Conversion is instantaneous but growth in grace takes time.) They are—we are—all flawed, and say and do things that appear to some to be not "Christian." As I grew in grace and knowledge I learned that I must accept people at face value and truly believe in them as individuals. Even if they are not, "living right" I must do my best to win them over, but not be upset if they reject what I say. Some of us are plagued with the "Messiah complex." This is when we think we are God and can do what only He can do. We sometimes carry the weight of this godless world on our shoulders thinking that we can change it. We in fact, can change only that which is in our sphere of influence through prayer and by our example.

I hope these stories and the thoughts I've shared about them have been a blessing to you. I myself have greatly benefited from them. I find hope as I see the struggles and the breakthroughs of these men of God. Through the years I have, and I know you have as well, faced many things that make you scratch your head and wonder, "God, are you out there, and if You are, where are You, and what are You doing?" Remember that Job really didn't need to know why, he needed God. After my accident I asked, "Why?" —I didn't get answers. But what I did get was a whole lot of love from His body who are His people. So many came and prayed for me. They didn't come with answers but with God's love. *God's love!* The heart screams, "Do you really *love* me God, really?"

As I have done this study my eyes have been opened more to the truth of God's word concerning suffering and pain, and to God's ultimate answer, which is, "I understand, I am with you and *I love you*." When things are good we don't think much about God's love or His truth concerning pain and suffering, but when things go south, that is when we ponder.

"...a thick and dreadful darkness came over him" (Gen 15:12). The book *Streams in the Desert*, by L.B. Cowman, has been one of those books that has hit me in the depths of my soul. In response to this verse she writes.

> "In this Scripture passage, the sun had fi-
> nally gone down, and the eastern night
> had swiftly cast its heavy veil over the en-
> tire scene. Worn out by the mental conflict,
> and the exertion and the cares of the day,
> Abraham, fell into a deep sleep. During
> his sleep, his soul was oppressed with a
> thick and dreadful darkness which seemed
> to smother him and felt like a nightmare in
> his heart. Do you have an understanding of

the horror of that kind of darkness? Have
you ever experienced a terrible sorrow that
seems difficult to reconcile with God's perfect love—a sorrow that comes crashing
down upon you, wrings from your soul its
peaceful rest in the grace of God, and casts
it into a sea of darkness that is unlit be even
one ray of hope? Have you experienced a
sorrow caused by unkindness, when others
cruelly mistreat your trusting heart, and
you even begin to wonder if there really is
a God above who sees what is happening
yet continues to allow it? If you know this
kind of sorrow, then you know something
of this, thick and dreadful darkness".

I am going to finish what she writes, quoting another author, and I want you to truly ponder your
heart, to the depths of your soul, when you read the
rest.

"Human life is made of brightness and
gloom, shadows and sunshine, and dark
clouds followed by brilliant rays of light.
Yet through it all, God's divine justice is ac-
complishing His plan, affecting and disciplining each individual soul. Dear friend,
if you are filled with fear of thick and
dreadful darkness because of God's dealings with humankind, learn to trust His
infallible wisdom, for it is equal to His un-
changing justice. And know that He who

endured the dreadful darkness of Calvary
and the feeling of having been forsaken
on the cross is ready to accompany you
through the valley of the shadow of death
(Ps 23:4) until you can see the sun shining
on the other side. May we realize that we
have this hope as an anchor for the soul,
firm and secure that it enters the inner sanctuary behind the curtain (Heb 6:19). And
may we know that although it is unseen
within His sanctuary, our anchor will be
grounded and will never yield. It will hold
firm until the day He returns, and then we
too will follow it into the safe haven guar-
anteed to us in God's unchangeable Word.
F.B. Meyer" [minister and writer].

She continues,

"The disciples thought that the angry sea
separated them from Jesus. In fact, some
of them thought something even worse—
they thought that the trouble they were
facing was a sign that He had forgotten
them and did not care about them. O dear
friend, that is when your troubles can cause
the most harm. The Devil comes and whis-
pers to you, 'God has forgotten you or God
has forsaken you,' and your unbelieving
heart cries out, as Gideon once did, 'If the
Lord is with us, why has all this happened

to us?' (Judges 6:13). God has allowed the difficulty to come upon you, in order to bring you closer to Himself. It has come not to separate you from Jesus but to cause you to cling to Him more faithfully, more firmly, and more simply. F. S. Webster [another minister and writer she quotes]. We should abandon ourselves to God more fully at those times when He seems to have abandoned us. Let us enjoy His light and comfort when it is His pleasure to give it to us, but may we not attach ourselves to His gifts. May we instead attach ourselves to Him, and when He plunges us into the night, where pure faith is required, may we still press on through the agonizing darkness".

This I believe summarizes what I have been trying to say. With all the talk of faith and what it really is and how it really works, I hope these stories and thoughts help you to see a couple things. One is that faith is for a lifetime. It constitutes a walk over a lifetime of ups and downs. If you see faith as only a means of getting things from God, you will be disappointed in the long run. Getting things from God by faith has to do with temporal issues that may or may not lead you to more of Him. Many have been greatly disappointed when what they had faith for never materialized. They gave time and money in hopes that what they were asking for, God would give. They saw giving money and time to God as payment for their answers, but after much time and money they saw no answers and eventually lost their faith.

This leads us to what faith is really supposed to do, which is to bring us more of Him. But what does that mean? More feeling, more morality, more mental energy, more inspiration? It may include these, and if God is at work in us, it will produce good fruit. "For it is God who works in you both to will and to do for His good pleasure" (Phil 2:13). Through this working, things will happen—and they should. We should become more loving, kind, patient and all the fruits of the spirit listed in Galatians chapter five. Yes, we should feel God closer to us but these feelings can be very subjective. One person feels one thing, another feels something different. Feelings are hard to put into a category to be able to say, "Yes, this is from God." Many fall victim to always using their feelings to judge if God is really with them. So, real faith is rooted in who God is. True faith is only as good as our understanding of God. Many have faith in who they believe God is, whether it is Mormon, Muslim, Hindu or any of the other various religions or schools of thought that express themselves as coming from God.

So those who accept these concepts of God have faith in what they believe. The question comes back to: Is what they believe real and true? This again brings us full circle back to what is written in the Bible. If we accept what is written as God breathed and inspired by Him then our only quest is to study and interpret it properly. "For whatever things were written before were written for our learning, that we, through the patience and comfort of the scriptures, might have hope" (Rom 15:4). In other words, when we read about men of faith in the Old Testament we learn what faith is. Jacob walked with God, and over his lifetime heard God speak at strategic times and did what God said. He was not a "good" man. He was a deceiver, but God used him and changed him over time. *Time.* This is the big thing associated with faith. Notice that, "… we, through the *patience* and comfort of the scriptures, might have hope." Patience is not something we are born with, it is a learned character trait that is burned into us as we walk by faith and trust in God. In reference to Jacob and his encounter with God, Cowman applies this to us.

> "Is God leading you in this way? Is this the meaning of your mysterious trial, your difficult circumstances, your impossible situation, or that trying place you cannot seem to move past without Him? But do you have enough of Him to win the victory?".

The life of faith is filled with hard places and more comfortable places. We like the easy and don't like the hard times. But we have been programmed by media and our culture to see rain as bad, to see no purpose in trials, and to see all the negative things in life that want to beat us down as having no value. Yet rain brings cleansing and life. The hard places in your life are designed to perfect your faith. "I tell you that He will avenge them [the elect who have faith] speedily. Nevertheless when the Son of Man comes will He find faith on the earth?" (Lk 18:8). If Jesus is looking for faith when He comes back, then I think that faith is one of the most important elements of our life. Faith is vital, without it we cannot please God. Hear what the writer of Hebrews says. (Many think it is Paul, but we don't know for sure because there is no signature.)

> "Now faith is the substance of things hoped for, the evidence of things not seen. For by it the elders obtained a good testimony. By faith we understand that the worlds were framed by the word of God, so that the things which are seen were not made of things which are visible. By faith Abel offered to God a more excellent sacrifice than Cain, through which he obtained witness that he was righteous, God testifying of his gifts; and through it he being dead still speaks. By faith Enoch was taken away so that he did not see death, 'and was not found, because God had taken him'; for before he was taken he had this testimony, that he pleased God. But without faith it is impossible to please Him, for he who comes to God must believe that He is, and that He is a rewarder of those who diligently seek Him" (Heb 11:1-6).

This passage is the most used passage among those who stress faith. Faith is seen as a means to a reward in many cases. The men we talked about as well as the men listed in the rest of this chapter had faith—but no where are they naming and claiming things. I heard a woman say the other day that someone she knew had died. She said if she would have known that she had authority over death at the time, (she had recently learned that she did) the person would not have died. This is just one misleading aspect of faith that is set forth by those who emphasize faith. Not that we should not pray for those who are sick that they should be made well—we should. (In my case, my friend Dr. Carl Bandalin told me that the night my crash happened, he was deeply impressed to pray, though he did not know for whom. He pulled his car over and prayed late into the night until, as he found out later, I stabilized early in the morning.)

But this idea that we have the power over death is taking faith to the extreme. Faith is the substance (hypostasis) of things hoped for. What does this mean? *Hypostasis* is a Greek word meaning the underlying or essential part of anything as distinguished from attributes, according to *Dictionary.com*. When you think of substance you think of something concrete, something actual. Regarding *"the evidence of things not seen"*, we have not seen God; we have not seen Him make anything—including the world around us. But faith sees the evidence of what has been made. It's like seeing a painting, knowing that someone had to have painted it. You have not seen the painting being made, but you see the evidence, the substance of what is and conclude that the painting has been made by someone. By faith you accept that what you see has been made, has indeed been made by someone. That is faith. You cannot believe in God without faith. To question your faith in God is really an oxymoron. It is like questioning your existence. Do I exist? You would have to exist to ask that question. Is red, red? Of course it is. It can be no other. Do you have faith in God? Do you believe in God? If you do, then you have faith. The next question is, God who? The God that Abraham, Isaac and Jacob believed in is the God who created all things, and is the same God who spoke (and still speaks) to and had (and still has) a plan and a purpose for the human family. This was the God in whom the Old Testament patriarchs believed. Their faith was not static, but dynamic. They accepted God as Creator of all things as well as the God who spoke to them, directed them and was personal with them.

Learn from these men, exercise patience in the God of the universe. When you're up lift other people up who may be down. When you're down know that God has not forsaken you, but is perfecting you. It's not easy, and as I look back at thirty years of walking with God, there were great times economically, physically, and spiritually. In these times I could rejoice and my faith seemed strong. When I was hit by a drunk driver and paralyzed from the waist down, I had faith to be completely healed at first. It has been over six years now and I still cannot walk without braces and crutches. I still need a miracle and I still believe that

God can do great things—though at times I wonder if it will ever happen. I wonder if I should, like many others, accept this as my life.

I met a Pastor's wife who had many physical problems who said a prayer every morning, and when she told me of it, it helped me. "Lord You could heal me today, but if You don't, I will still love and serve You." This prayer reveals that God is powerful and sovereign. God could, at any time, heal anyone—and He does heal people. But if healing does not come in the way we think it should, we should still determine to love and trust God. I told a young man the other day who was struggling with seeing the world in a biblical way. "Why do bad people prosper and good people struggle?" This was the gist of what he was thinking. I tried to encourage him to believe in God outside of what he sees. This is difficult, especially for young people. They are still in this transition time from child to adult. Each person is at a different level and matures at different times in different ways. Jesus was thirty when He started His ministry, and when I think about this it helps me be more patient with the younger generation. It takes time. Jacob was a young, manipulative, and bound by many things. Outwardly he was not what you would consider "Christian" but God had a plan and a purpose for this young man. I believe we can apply this to every young person today. It may have nothing to do with starting a nation, but it is a real purpose. Some would disagree and say Jacob has nothing to do with us and applying this to us is a mistake. This is where good people disagree and it is okay. I choose to believe and I think I stand on scriptural grounds that we can learn from people of faith and apply it to ourselves. God knows each person individually and generally wants the best for each person in terms of health and wealth, but there is something that is more important than these—and that is faith till the end no matter what.

Some say that faith is a gift from God. If you believe this, then you would have to say that God gives some people faith and withholds it from others, which makes God the author of unbelief. I don't think this lines up with the character of God. God will not cause some to believe and others not. In fact, this goes against the concept of will, and makes us subject to believing against our own will. The adage applies here: God did not make us robots. The other extreme is that faith is simply a choice that we make on the same level as choosing what to eat for dinner, or what car to buy. I do not think it is quite that simple either.

Here is an analogy. A young man is about his business and doing just fine. He is single until one day he sees a beauty; a young woman who captures his attention. His whole insides are affected by what he sees, but not only is she beautiful externally, there is an attraction that calls him. She makes it plain by her actions that she is available and she is attracted to him as well. She is not just another pretty face; she is different. The timing is just right and she may even—if she is bold enough—seek him out. She eventually captures his heart and he agrees to marry her and spend the rest of his life with her. We don't often think of God like this, but Paul said that it is, "Or do you despise the riches of His goodness, forbearance and long-suffering, not knowing that the goodness of God leads you to repentance" (Rom 2:4). The goodness of God is what leads a person to repentance. Just like the kindness of a woman or man may lead one to embrace them for life. This may be how it happens for some. For others it may happen differently, as in my case—I was afraid of going to hell...(for not repenting before God I mean—not for not marrying my wife!)

I felt guilty about my actions and behavior. I did not feel as if God was "wooing" me to Himself, I felt extreme conviction about my actions and rebellion. My inward eyes were open to my heart and why I was acting the way I was. I was not just "having a good time," I was in stark rebellion to the God of the universe. Looking back, it was God's mercy, love and beauty that were calling, but at the time I did not see that; I only saw my sin and what I needed to do—which was to seek Him while He was calling me, which gratefully, I did. This is a far cry from making a decision about what color to paint the bathroom; it was far more radical than that. Faith actually came to me by hearing the word of God, and is sustained by continuing to listen to God and His word (Rom 10:17). So faith comes to us as we respond to God's word. Faith begins with God, not us. God makes it available to all, He convicts the world—which means everyone. Many are called, few are chosen (Matt 20:16). In essence all are called and only a few are chosen because only a few choose. The word responsibility means having the ability to respond. This is God's gift, an ability to respond to truth and be changed. The first response to God is the first step in the journey of a lifetime. This is the beginning of your faith walk. You are now aware of the spirit world and are commanded to move ahead in your understanding and love of God. This is the first commandment, "Jesus said to him, 'You shall love the Lord your God with all your heart, with all your soul and with all your mind. This is the first and great commandment'" (Matt 22:37-38). This is not as easy as it sounds, especially when hard times come.

You may be just beginning your walk of faith. Perhaps you recently accepted Jesus as your Lord and are alive and feel good about your decision to walk by faith and not by sight. You will face many things and your faith will be challenged by "various trials" (James 1:2). Know that this is by divine design. "Keep your heart with all diligence, for out of it spring the issues of life" (Prov 4:23). You will be tempted to question God when hard times come. Everything in you will cry out, "God why? and God what…?" I want to tell you that's alright, it will be alright, just keep walking. Learn from these men. Those of you who have been walking for a period of time know that this is a lifelong journey, and hopefully by reading this book you have been encouraged. Here is a verse that has come to mean a great deal to me and I will leave it with you as I close this book.

"Have you not known? Have you not heard? The everlasting God, the Lord, the Creator of the ends of the earth, neither faints nor is weary, His understanding is unsearchable. He gives power to the weak, and to those who have no might He increases strength. Even youths shall faint and be weary, and the young men shall utterly fall, but those who wait on the Lord shall renew their strength; they shall mount up with wings like eagles, they shall run and not be weary, they shall walk and not faint" (Is 40:28-31).

Bibliography

The author quotes liberally from the following, and recommends these works to the reader:

1. Gregory A. Boyd, *Is God to Blame?: Beyond Pat Answers to the Problem of Suffering* (Downers Grove: InterVarsity Press, 2003).

2. L.B. Cowman, *Streams in the Desert* (Grand Rapids: Zondervan, 2006).

3. Dr. Timothy Johnson, *Finding God in the Questions: A Personal Journey* (Downers Grove: InterVarsity Press, 2004).

4. Harold S. Kushner, *When Bad Things Happen to Good People* (New York: Random House, Inc., 1980).

5. John Piper, Justin Taylor, eds. *Suffering and the Sovereignty of God* (Wheaton: Crossway Books & Bibles, 2006).

6. Ruth A. Tucker, *God Talk: Cautions for Those Who Hear God's Voice* (Downers Grove: InterVarsity Press, 2006).